GARDENS FOR ALL SEASONS

GARDENS FOR ALL SEASONS

by Jack Kramer

Photographs by Max Eckert
Drawings by Carol Carlson

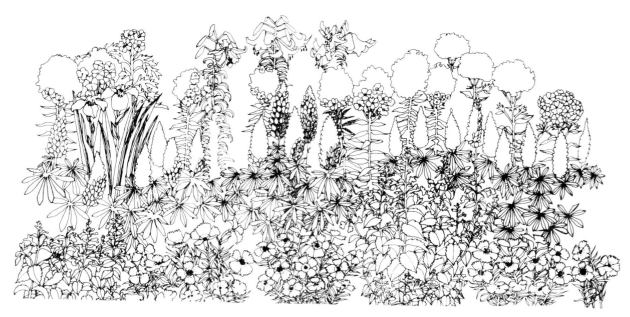

HARRY N. ABRAMS, INC., PUBLISHERS, NEW YORK

Project Manager: Margaret L. Kaplan

Editor: Ellyn Childs Allison

Designer: Linda D. Schifano

Library of Congress Cataloging in Publication Data

Kramer, Jack, 1927–
  Gardens for all seasons.

  Bibliography: p.201
  Includes index.
  1. Landscape gardening — United States. 2. Gardens
— United States. 3. Gardens — Design. I. Title.
SB473.K733   712'.6   81-2377
ISBN 0-8109-0951-0   AACR2

Published in 1981 by Harry N. Abrams, Incorporated, New York

Printed and bound in Japan

CONTENTS

PREFACE &
ACKNOWLEDGMENTS

In all my years of reading and writing about gardening, I have never come across a book on seasonal gardening. It seemed to me that a volume of photographs, drawings, and information on gardens around the United States in each of the four seasons of the year would be of great interest, and the idea of writing one was challenging. Thus *Gardens for All Seasons* was born.

Of course I never considered why no such book had ever been published. Now, after 40,000 miles of travel and three years of battling the logistics of weather in eight states across the country, I find the answer only too apparent. Catching nature on film in a specific place at a specific time is a complex, often frustrating task. But we did finally succeed in capturing a variety of gardens for all seasons in the photographs you see here. I sincerely hope you will find in this book all the information and inspiration you need to make your own garden beautiful all year round.

I wish to thank the owners of all the gardens we illustrate here. No doubt it was a bother to them—to have photographers scurrying about your garden every three months is no joy. But they all gave us much encouragement and were full of enthusiasm for the project. To each and every one of them I want to express my deepest gratitude.

My photographer Max Eckert is a man who works with nature on a grand scale—and his patience is extraordinary: on one occasion he waited to take photos for three days until it stopped raining. The number of hours he clocked in the air in pursuit of seasonal beauty would seem to entitle him to a free ticket on the cross-country airlines.

My gratitude is, again, due to the artist Carol Carlson, who is responsible for the excellent drawings in this book.

1. A GARDEN FOR YOU

A pleasing garden is more than a collection of plants growing haphazardly in an outdoor area. It is an aesthetic expression created the way a painter composes a landscape painting. It should solace the soul and delight the eye in any season.

Gardens may be formal, informal, or, as in most cases, a combination of both styles. A formal plan is geometrically balanced. If there is a tree on the right, for example, then there will probably be a tree on the left, and square, rectangular, oval, and circular lawns and beds will provide an orderly look.

In an informal scheme the plantings are more casual-looking and asymmetrical. There may be three trees on one side of the house and two on the other, and flowers may appear in curved drifts rather than in regular beds. Clumps of wildflowers or native shrubs growing naturally can become the focal point of the garden, or if there are none they can be planted.

Just what kind of garden style you choose depends upon such factors as the topography of the site, the architectural style of the house, the size of the property, the use to which the garden will be put, and, of course, your own preferences. Hilly topography usually calls for a natural planting scheme, whereas a level site is handled best in a more formal way. Rooftops usually cannot accommodate large trees and shrubs, so flowers must create the colorful yearly cycle. Look at our photographs of the Bergeson garden in San Francisco to see how seasonal pot plants almost single-handedly create a lovely twelve-month picture. Even the smallest backyard can become a charming four-season retreat with color abounding. The

Backed by lush green ferns, this display of mums in pots and a hanging basket creates dramatic fall color in the Milo Scott Bergesons' San Francisco roof garden.

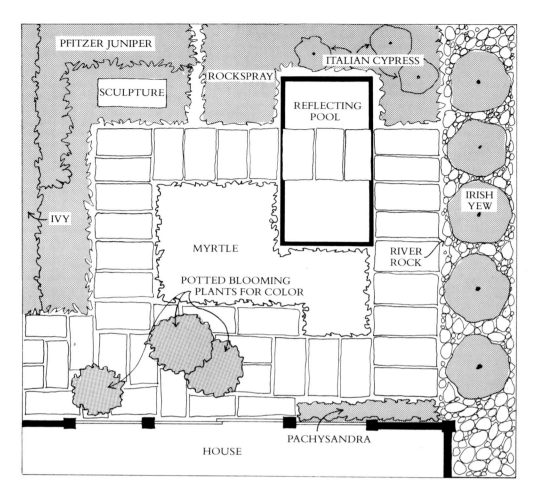

PFITZER JUNIPER

ITALIAN CYPRESS

ROCKSPRAY

SCULPTURE

REFLECTING
POOL

IVY

IRISH
YEW

MYRTLE

RIVER
ROCK

POTTED BLOOMING
PLANTS FOR COLOR

PACHYSANDRA

HOUSE

Dannhausen garden in Chicago, for example, is truly a country estate in miniature. If you have ample grounds, you can develop a garden of great variety and distinction. For example, several small gardens can interact to become the whole garden. In the Banks garden in Atlanta and the Stone garden in Charlottesville, plantings of different types at different levels make a wonderfully diversified yet harmonious picture.

Your garden should always be designed to work for you, to adapt to the kind of life you live. If you love flowers in the house or the taste and scent of fresh herbs, plant a cutting garden or herb garden somewhere on your grounds. These gardens can be small—even windowbox-size, if necessary. If you and your family enjoy sitting out in the winter sunshine, you can plant a garden of evergreens and early-flowering shrubs and bulbs in a sunny, well-protected spot. If you would rather not rake leaves, use evergreens instead of deciduous trees to provide coolness and shade. The variety of gardens and garden plans is almost limitless. With thought and careful preparation you can enjoy the one that is perfect for you.

LANDSCAPE SYMBOLS

Deciduous

Hedge

Evergreen

Potted plant

Ground cover

Miscellaneous plants

Cultivated

Fence

Stone paving

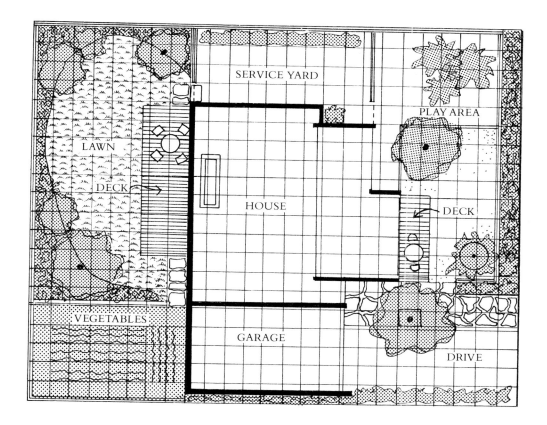

Begin with Preliminary Sketches

After studying the sample plans scattered through this book, look at your property and decide where your garden should be. You might have one garden or a combination—a backyard and a side garden, perhaps, the **L**-shaped garden. It helps to make sketches of the area showing existing trees and shrubs. Or, if you are starting from scratch, mark where you want to put flower beds, trees, and shrubs. An exact sketch is not necessary. Choose simple symbols for types of plants—a circle for a tree, a cross for a shrub—and indicate the outline of a flower bed. Shade in green areas with a pencil. Think now about where the sun will fall at different times of year and about the shade that large trees and bushes will cast. Shade and sun are important factors to consider when you locate flower beds and choose plants to grow in them. (Most plants need some sun, many require a lot; your local nurseryman or a garden catalogue can tell you how much.)

Once you have the sketch completed, you can determine propor-

Opposite:
The attractiveness of this green, green garden on the William Nathaniel Banks estate in Atlanta is partly the result of a tiered spatial arrangement. Note that the plants are also placed at different levels to achieve a layered look.

A lush green lawn and well-kept trees and shrubs are the bone structure of this handsome ornamental garden on the Whitney Stone estate in Charlottesville.

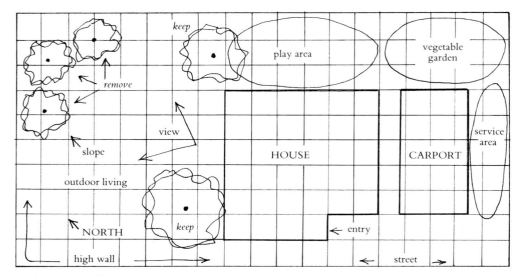

Preliminary plan

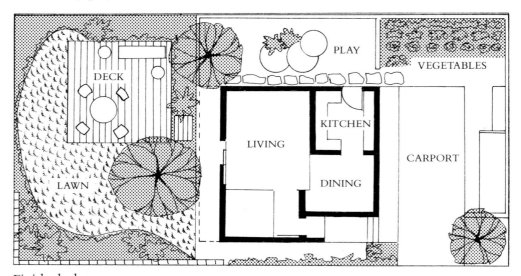

Finished plan

tion and balance and get an overall idea of how your garden will look. Make several sketches until you find one that pleases you. As in a painting, the parts should be harmonious and create a unity. Consider the basic types of gardens described in Chapter Three. You will probably want to include one or more of these in your master plan. One way to find inspiration is to study your neighbors' gardens and combine their ideas with your own. Looking at their gardens will also help you to choose plants that thrive in your area. If you like, consult a landscape architect first about specific plans, and then about plant material. One or two consultations need not be expensive. A professional can do preliminary sketches for you or follow through with the entire garden.

14

FORM IN THE GARDEN:
RECTANGULAR

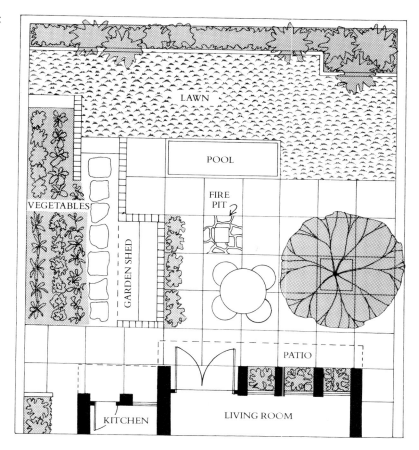

FORM IN THE GARDEN:
TRIANGULAR

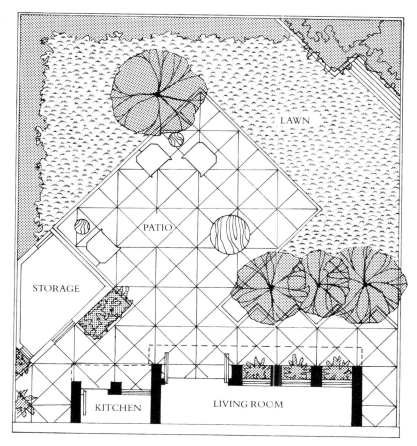

Choosing the Flowers

Now, with your master plan completed, you can fill in the detail for each season, making a list of bedding plants that will supply the color you want. A basic checklist would include the following types:

Annuals: Grown from seed or purchased as immature plants, the annuals' life span extends through one flowering season only. (The term has been expanded to include tender perennials that live through winter only in frost-free areas.) These are the plants that paint your garden with

Opposite:
If one had to name America's favorite bulb it would probably be the tulip. Swept together in masses, as here on the Whitney Stone estate in Charlottesville, they are breathtaking.

Left:
Zinnias, cosmos, and snapdragons vie with each other for attention in this handsome summer bed on the grounds of the vast garden of Mrs. Corydon Wagner in Tacoma. The evergreens in the background are a perfect foil for the flowers' color.

Hibiscus flowers always create a mood of gaiety.

16

carefree color, and you can easily experiment with them, trying different varieties each year.

Perennials and biennials: Started from seed or purchased as established plants, perennials are the mainstay of most garden beds. They return year after year where you first planted them, requiring little maintenance to keep them healthy and beautiful. Biennials can be started from seed like annuals but do not flower until the following year. Many gardeners prefer to purchase biennial seedlings in spring and bed them in like annuals. Many of our most beautiful flowers are biennials: pansies, for example, and Canterbury bells. Some reseed themselves and become as dependable as perennials.

Bulbs: Bulbs are the ugly ducklings of the garden. Each dull brown package contains a little flower (and the food to feed it) that will burst forth in a miracle of bloom after a season of rest. Some bulbs flower in spring, some in fall. Some must be dug up before frost or, like tulips, after a few years in the ground, and then dried and stored for later planting; others, like daffodils, come up year after year.

Most gardens planted for a spring scene are painted with the color of bulbs within a setting of shrubs or trees, or in beds. Tulips, for example, are the basis of the first-season show in Mrs. Wagner's garden in Tacoma. In the late spring and summer we rely on annuals and perennials after the bulbs have died down. They not only bring fresh bloom but conceal the leggy, sprawling foliage of bulbs past their flowering season. In Mrs. Wagner's garden, zinnias, marigolds, cosmos, and snapdragons draw a many-colored curtain on the tulips. Summer-flowering bulbs like the dahlias and lilies also fill in gaps left by earlier bloomers. In fall, some of the late

18

summer perennials will still be in flower, and more color comes with fall-blooming varieties. Red roses flower again in the Banks garden at the end of summer, providing a magnificent backdrop for white and yellow chrysanthemums. If you live in a cold climate, you must rely in winter on evergreens, late-flowering or berried shrubs, and the earliest bulbs. The landscape once again will be different, with rich, dark green and an occasional splash of bright color foretelling the beauty of spring to come. If, like the Getzes of Phoenix, you are lucky enough to live in a climate of mild winters, you can enjoy a blaze of summer color throughout the year.

In each season, annuals, perennials, biennials, and bulbs should go into the ground in good soil that is porous: give your plants the opportunity to live, not just exist. Soil is depleted of nutrients in the annual life cycle, so renew it frequently. After digging up any bulbs and perennials to protect them from damage, spade up six to ten inches of the old soil and mix it thoroughly with organic material (manure, compost, and peat moss are commonly used) and commercial fertilizer. If your plants are in containers, you can add purchased potting soil instead.

The lists in Chapter Five and at the back of this book give the color and blooming time of many garden plants, and in the next chapter you will find some suggestions for grouping colors to achieve pleasant seasonal effects. Finally, take a careful look at the gardens from various parts of the United States shown in this book in their four-season beauty—in spring, summer, fall, and winter. They are inspiring. Borrow ideas from one or another as you plan your own. And keep in mind that the four-season garden will require a little more work and money than the two-season garden, but that it will be well worth it.

2. ORCHESTRATING THE COLORS IN A GARDEN

Most gardens sparkle with color during each season. Knowing how to blend different colors together harmoniously is one of the secrets of a successful gardener. Though it is not difficult to arrive at pleasing combinations by experimentation—and you certainly will want to experiment —it is also helpful to keep in mind a few formulas that have proved to work well in every kind of garden.

Color Primer

First let us look at the different color groups, for each color affects us differently, by itself and in combination with others. Warm colors, such as red and orange, have an intense effect, brilliant and exciting; blue and white are cool and calming. As leading colors blues and whites tend to give formality to a garden, and they should be used in masses. If reds and oranges are the leaders, use them judiciously—just a few of them—or they will overpower both scene and viewer. A few drifts are enough. Yellow has much of the warmth of red but lacks its violence. It is a cheerful color and a wonderful mixer, blending well with the reds and oranges as well as the blues and purples.

Blue to Purple: Blue is a receding color that gives a serene character to a

Here is an example of intelligent color planning. The spectrum moves gradually from orange to yellow and then is repeated. There are no jarring effects but many subtle ones.

garden. Blue flowers convey a sense of distance and space and will tone down strong pinks and oranges. Because blue flowers offer perhaps the greatest variation in shade, it is important to select blue flowering plants with care. Be especially alert when placing blue next to red. The wrong shade can create havoc. On the other hand, the right shade (often a blue-gray) will soften the dazzling effect that scarlet or pure red has on the eye. Because the green of foliage looks cool, and most gardens without flowers already give a cool impression, a garden of cool colors only is usually not successful. The exception comes in the fall, when cool colors harmonize well with a brilliant background of autumn foliage.

Pink to Rose: Pink is a pastel color—heavenly to look at and exquisite in the garden. Pink can be elusive and delicate. Flowering peach, plum, and cherry trees in bloom are clouds of color. Light pinks and darker pink colors combine beautifully with white. Nothing more may be needed. Pink holds its own with blue and makes blue more appealing in the land-scape. Pale pink and lavender make a splendid combination, very restful in the heat of summer. The rose shades, somewhat darker, are equally at home in the garden. If not as delicate as pink, they combine beautifully with blue and provide high contrast, which is often needed in a garden. However, these flowers must be placed together carefully or they may create a jarring effect.

Red: Red is a strong color. Red flowers bring excitement to the garden. They come in many different shades, some brilliant and fiery, others more subdued, so select them carefully. To many people, the stimulation of red is eventually tiring, and it is often a good idea to tone down red flowers by placing them near blue blossoms or, for a startling but pleasing effect, near white ones. Use them as the garnish—the accent—and they will provide marvelous effects. But, if you are sure of your taste, give it free rein and let them take over the garden. This spring border, which dances with reds of all shades, is as dramatic as a bravura performance of *Carmen*.

SPRING GARDEN

1. Peach trees (*Prunus persica* 'Cardinal')

2. Weigela bushes (*Weigela* 'Bristol Ruby')

3. Quince bushes (*Cydonia oblonga* 'Spitfire')

4. Azalea bushes (*Rhododendron*, Exbury hybrid)

5. Tulips (*Tulipa* 'Orange Favorite')

6. English primroses (*Primula acaulis* hybrid)

7. Anemones (*Anemone fulgens annulata grandiflora*)

8. Hyacinths (*Hyacinthus orientalis* 'Jan Bos')

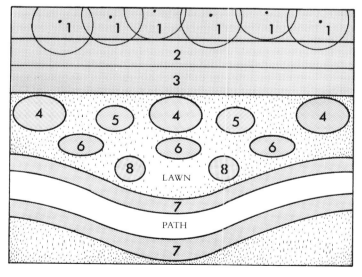

Grape hyacinths, phlox, and tulips—
flowers of different shapes—are com-
bined in the Eldon Dannhausen garden
in Chicago in an interesting and beautiful
way. There is no monotony here.

Yellow to Orange: Yellow is the basic color in most gardens. First of all, yellow signals spring—bursting out in daffodils and crocuses, for example. But yellow flowers are also splendid in summer, looking their best in the full sunshine of July and August, and they are almost mandatory in the fall. There is a shade of yellow compatible with almost every other hue, and with touches of white, sky-blue, and deep purple, yellow-orange flowers make a dazzling border display. Whether in a mixed border or in specimen plants, yellow is an excellent outdoor color, not only vibrant when the sun is shining but still warm on dull days. There are so many flowers of different tones of yellow (through bronze and gold to orange) that it is possible to have yellow in the garden all year long until frost, and its bright, cheerful note will create combinations with other flower colors that are appealing and never monotonous.

White: White always creates a cooling effect and enhances the color of any neighboring plant. In addition, white flowers are an especially effective means of balancing cool and warm shades, and they create a unity that is desirable in landscaping. In masses and drifts, white is sure to provide a look of elegance, and a predominantly white-and-blue garden can be a show stopper. If the garden is full of many different colors, then the white drifts should be repeated in several places so that the white flowers will hold their own and carry out their unifying role. White flowers are visible after dark, and you will enjoy their shimmer by a pool or patio on hot summer evenings.

Green: The most important color in your garden will probably be green, which acts as a canvas for all the other colors. Even the city gardener, who works chiefly with pots and hanging baskets, relies upon the green of plant foliage to soften the vibrant effect of scarlet petunias or yellow chrysanthemums against brick walls and white containers, for green is most restful to the eye. The tints of green in the leaves and needles of plants fill a vast spectrum, from the palest silver-green of the dusty miller plant to

Left:
In one of Mrs. Corydon Wagner's gardens in Tacoma, white impatiens makes a handsome statement against a rich green background. The topiary swan seems to swim in white foam.

Delicate shades of yellow, pink, and white are the basis of this scene in the Leola B. Fraim garden near Boston. Note the spicy accent—a touch of purple.

the deep tones of yew trees and boxwood bushes. Working with a palette of green, you can enrich your shady garden areas. Ferns and evergreens make havens of coolness where flowers will not grow. If you live in a region of severe or even moderate winters, the green of foliage, set off by red splashes of berries and the white of snow, will bring color to your garden throughout the fourth, darkest season of the year.

Planning for Color in Four Seasons

Color can be described not only by hue (red, blue, purple, blue-green, etc.) but by value and intensity. Value is the measure of light in a color, and, while hue is important in planning a garden, value is more important. Intensity is the purity of a color. The less it contains of its complement, the purer or more intense a color is. You will put all these attributes of color into action in designing your garden. The palette of colors you choose to work with may be very large, or you may decide on a narrower range (for example, pinks, roses, lavenders, whites).

Make a list of the flowers you love in each season and their colors (the lists in the back of the book will be helpful). Now, keeping your master garden plan in mind—whether it calls for a single border of flowers or a sweeping vista of trees and shrubs as well as beds—try to establish for each season's display a balance in the whole picture your eye will encounter. Balance can be achieved by grouping hues, values, and intensities of color so they blend pleasantly together and make a unified statement.

One of the easiest ways of achieving a sense of unity is to choose one predominant color in each season and distribute it across the entire garden, prominently but not in an overpowering way. By using gradations of value you can avoid a spotty effect. You might place light values of your leading color close by and dark values in the distance, to make a rhythmic sequence, or move the other way, from dark to light. Working in steps will smooth the sequence. If you start with the lightest value, move on to a smaller amount of medium value, and then to an equally diminished amount of the darkest. In this way there will be character in your color scheme that will not fade away when seen from a distance.

Though rules exist only to be broken, bear in mind when establishing your master color plan that, when used to accent each other, warm and cool colors should usually be related in value and intensity. Thus, pale blue and pale yellow always work well together; dark blue and pale yellow may not, because a marked difference in value can unsettle a complex chromatic scheme running through a garden.

You can also work in sequences of warm to cool and the reverse. Start with red, work into orange-red, orange, orange-yellow, yellow, and finally into white. Or work the other way, from white to blue-pink or rose-pink, into near-red and red. In such sequences, sudden contrasts give a sparse effect, unpleasing to the eye. So if you are using a full warm-to-cool sequence of color gradations along a bed or into the distance, be sure you have enough space to do it—at least 150 feet. If you lack space for the full run, having only, say, 50 feet, then plan to use not more than a third of the scale.

When planning your color schemes, remember that the color of any architecture or furniture that will be seen in conjunction with your plants should harmonize with them. The heights of the plants you choose will also have a bearing on their placement, and balancing their shapes is important, too. (It is pleasant to mix round-headed with spiky flowers, for example.) Planning a colorful garden can be as simple or as complicated as you want to make it. The task is always delightful, and it need never come to an end, for gardens, like plants, tend to grow, spread, and flourish as the years pass.

3. KINDS OF GARDENS

Your garden may be strictly for looking at or it may be a working garden, producing cut flowers for the house or vegetables for the kitchen. It may be large and contain several gardens within it, or small—only a border with a few shrubs. It may be a rooftop or a small backyard in the city. There are infinite variations, and our photographs show some of the possibilities.

Ornamental Gardens

The viewing or ornamental garden is both beautiful to see and a physical asset. Besides giving comfort to the spirit it enhances the value of a house. The garden with which we are most familiar, it relies on trees and shrubs as a framework. There are usually (but not always) flowers, a lawn or lawns, and paths or walks to make the garden a usable area. The largest category of garden, it can be expanded in the country to include specialized gardens, or in the city it may become a tiny, jewellike setting for a handful of shrubs and flowers.

In any garden that relies on many trees and shrubs for its beauty, pruning and trimming are important chores. Certain trees benefit by topping from time to time so that light will penetrate the foliage (this is best done by professionals). Others, like the spruces, will not stand topping;

The effect of flowers displayed in arcs and curves is formal, yet graceful. Here, vivid color contrasts create a dramatic picture.

instead, lower branches may be removed to achieve the same result. Shrubbery must be kept in bounds by clipping and trimming. Established lawns require periodic feeding, watering, and weeding. None of these tasks is particularly arduous; besides, they all provide an opportunity to spend time in the fresh air and sunshine.

Cutting Gardens

How wonderfully satisfying to have cosmos, snapdragons, lupines, and such in a place where you can snip and cut to your heart's content! The more flowers you cut, the more you get, because with most plants cutting encourages new bloom. And, because you will not be cutting all your flowers, a cutting garden can be part of an ornamental garden as well.

The bed need not be extensive. I have grown a crowd of annuals and perennials in an area no larger than a five-by-ten-foot planter bin. In this container flourished enough painted tongues, Peruvian lilies, stocks, and cosmos to fill the house with color. If space is at a premium (and it usually is), you can also consider a step or terrace garden. Such a garden utilizes space to the fullest and also provides easy access. Make the beds no more than three feet wide or they will be hard to tend. You can also plant annuals for cutting in the same bed as your carrots, zucchini, and peppers, for they like the same treatment as vegetables.

For a cutting garden of any size, prepare a rich blend of soil at least two feet deep. Select a sunny spot for your bed, of course: a southern or eastern exposure. And, if you can, put in a path or paths to make caring for the plants easier. Feed and water your plants adequately to keep them at peak health.

At the start spacing is important, because plants must have room enough to grow. Crowded conditions will not yield a bountiful harvest.

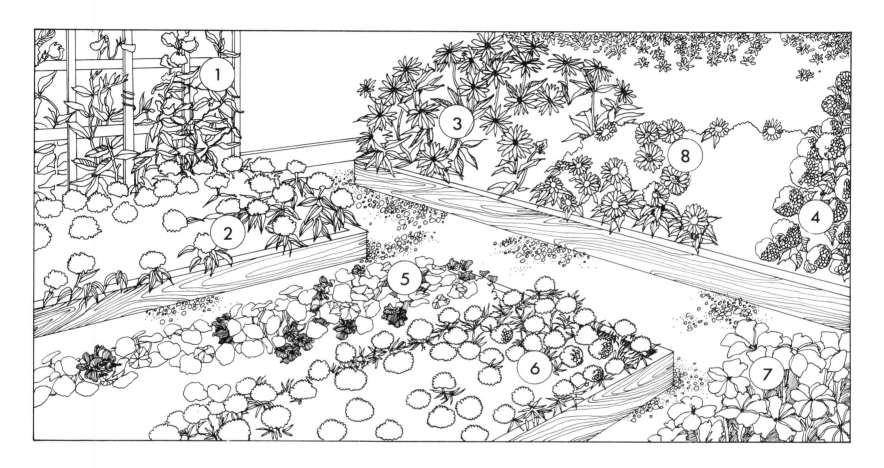

CUTTING GARDEN

1. Sweet peas (*Lathyrus odoratus* 'Spencer's Giant')

2. Sweet williams (*Dianthus barbatus*)

3. Gloriosa daisies (*Rudbeckia*)

4. Dahlias (Pompon type)

5. Nasturtiums (*Tropaeolum* 'Glorious Gleam')

6. Marigolds (*Tagetes erecta* 'Cream Puff')

7. Painted tongues (*Salpiglossis sinuata* 'Splash')

8. Shasta daisies (*Chrysanthemum maximum* 'Thomas Killin')

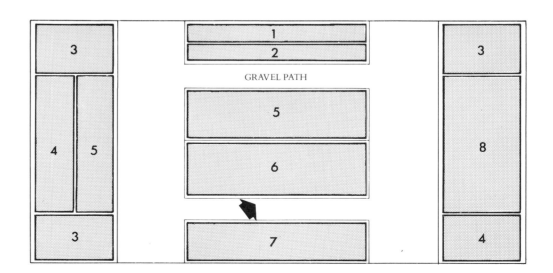

Above:
All the concepts of good garden planning are in evidence in this corner of the Whitney Stone garden in Charlottesville: variety, pleasing proportion, and a masterful balance of shapes and colors.

There are hundreds of zinnias here—enough to cut for a mansion and still have dozens left.

You can plant in drifts or arcs rather than straight lines, but if visual appeal is not especially important to you, straight rows will do just as well. If possible, align your bed in a north-south direction to give each plant an equal share of sun. You want enough plants to produce really abundant bloom, so use at least a few dozen of one kind here, another group of another kind there, and so on. It is wise to separate annuals and biennials from bulbs and perennials, which need room and do not like to be disturbed during the growing season. As in your border garden, plant for a succession of bloom: bulbs and annuals for spring; annuals, perennials, and bulbs for summer; perennials and bulbs for fall. Many people prefer the simplicity of a cutting garden composed of spring and summer annuals alone, letting their cutting garden rest in fall and winter; if you are one of them, be sure to plant some of the everlastings to keep summer in your house through the fall and winter months while your garden sleeps. Strawflowers and ornamental grasses dry beautifully and make colorful four-season arrangements.

Of course, some flowers stay colorful longer than others, and these are the ones to concentrate on. For your cutting garden I suggest these flowers:

ANNUALS
African daisy (*Arctotis*)
Baby's breath (*Gypsophila elegans*)
Cape marigold (*Dimorphotheca pluvialis*)
China aster (*Callistephus chinensis*)
Cosmos
*Globe amaranth (*Gomphrena globosa*)
Larkspur (*Consolida ambigua*)
Lupine (*Lupinus hartwegii*)
Mignonette (*Reseda odorata*)
Painted tongue (*Salpiglossis sinuata*)
Pincushion flower (*Scabiosa atropurpurea*)
Pink (*Dianthus*)
Pot marigold (*Calendula officinalis*)
Snapdragon (*Antirrhinum*)
*Strawflower (*Helichrysum bracteatum*)
Sunflower (*Helianthus*)
*Sunrays (*Helipterum roseum*)
Vervain (*Verbena*)
Zinnia (*Zinnia elegans*)

PERENNIALS & BULBS
Blanket flower, or gaillardia
(*Gaillardia aristata*)
Chrysanthemum
Daffodil (*Narcissus*)
Dahlia
Edging candytuft (*Iberis sempervirens*)
Gloriosa daisy (*Rudbeckia*)
Hardy aster, or Michaelmas daisy
(*Aster novi-belgii*)
†Iris
Japanese anemone (*Anemone japonica*)
†Lily (*Lilium*)
Painted daisy (*Chrysanthemum coccineum*)
Peony (*Paeonia*)
Tickseed (*Coreopsis*)
†Tulip (*Tulipa*)
*Yarrow (*Achillea*)

---

* Grow for dried bouquets as well as for cutting.
† For a progression of bloom, plant several different varieties.

Herb Gardens

Herbs, like the everlasting annuals, are for all seasons. Dried and set aside in July and August, they bring the scents and flavors of summer into your home throughout the dark months of the year. Not only are herbs grown for cooking, many—lavender and rose geranium, for example—are enjoyed for fragrance in sachets and potpourris.

Herbs are attractive plants that are easy to grow in average conditions. They need take little space and can be grown in pots or directly in the ground in small beds. Put them near the kitchen so you can just step outside to snip fresh herbs for a stew or salad, and to enjoy a refreshing scent.

As the herbs tend to have similar foliage and growth habits, they adapt well to decorative bedding plans. Little edged beds strung together in a geometrical arrangement by small paths make a charming showcase for these low, fluffy plants. The herb garden on Mrs. Wagner's grounds in Tacoma is an extremely beautiful example of formal bedding.

Some herbs germinate easily and grow quickly from seed sown outdoors after the last frost. Others should be started from seed indoors in early spring or bought as small plants and bedded in when warm weather arrives. In general, these plants prefer soil that is somewhat sandy, draining readily, and most kinds must be in the sun for at least three hours a day. Keep the soil moist after the plants have gotten a start, and divide and prune the herbs occasionally to keep them within bounds and to prevent them from crowding each other out.

Fresh herbs can be used as needed. Cut them as their flowers are about to open, when the essential oils are most plentiful. To save herbs for future use, pick the leaves from the stems, wash them in cold water, and then dry them thoroughly by spreading them out over a wire mesh in a warm place. Or put them on a baking sheet in a 200-degree oven with the door open.

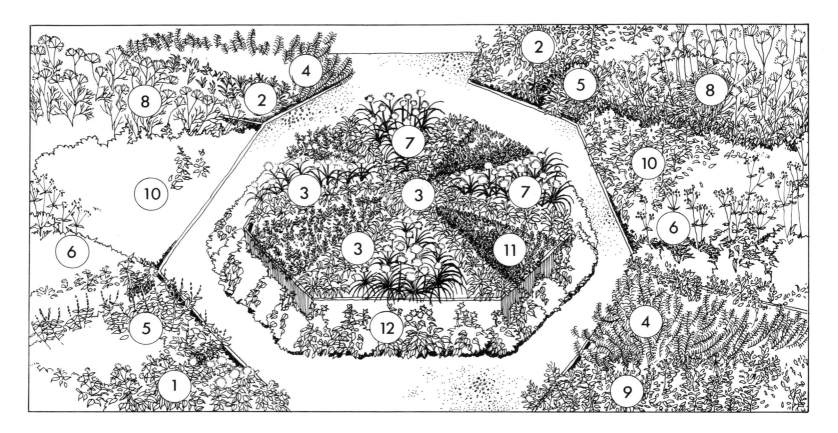

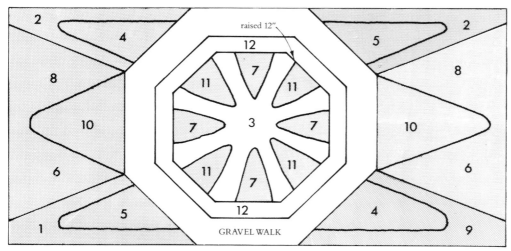

GRAVEL WALK

HERB GARDEN

1. Mint (*Mentha spicata*)

2. Tarragon (*Artemisia redowskii*)

3. Sage (*Salvia officinalis*)

4. Rosemary (*Rosmarinus officinalis*)

5. Sweet marjoram (*Majorana hortensis*)

6. Lovage (*Levisticum officinale*)

7. Chives (*Allium schoenoprasum*)

8. Dill (*Anethum graveolens*)

9. Oregano (*Origanum vulgare*)

10. Basil (*Ocimum basilicum*)

11. Thyme (*Thymus vulgaris*)

12. Borage (*Borago officinalis*)

Do not overdry the leaves; they should barely reach the crumbling stage. When they are dry, put them in airtight containers. To make a fragrant potpourri, pick and dry many rose petals—at least a quart. Add dried garden herbs: rose geranium, lemon verbena, lavender, rosemary, basil, mint. Spices from your kitchen shelf add zest: cinnamon, clove, allspice, mace. Mix all together and leave in a sealed container for several weeks. Stir occasionally. Orrisroot, which preserves the scent, is obtainable at most drugstores.

Herbs—a Garden Guide

Herb	Maximum ht. (in inches)	Sow seed outdoors	Buy plants	Special treatment	Use
*Basil	24	☐		Pinch plants back	Flavor soups, stews, tomato sauce; add to potpourris
*Borage	18	☐			Flavor salads, cool drinks
†Chives	6	☐	☐	Pot for winter use indoors	Flavor salads, soups, egg and cheese dishes
*Dill	36	☐	☐	Pot for winter use indoors	Flavor pickles, fish and egg dishes
†Lavender	30		☐		Scent sachets, potpourri
‡Lemon Verbena	30		☐	Pot for winter use indoors	Scent sachets, potpourri
†Mint	36	☐	☐	Keep plants contained in bed	Flavor cool drinks, jellies, vegetable dishes; add to potpourris
§Parsley	15	☐	☐	Pot for winter use indoors	Use as garnish and to flavor soups, stews, salads
‡Rose geranium	36		☐	Pot for winter use indoors	Flavor jellies, desserts; scent sachets, potpourris
‡Rosemary	48		☐	Pot for winter use indoors	Flavor salads, soups, stews; add to potpourris
†Sage	24	☐	☐		Flavor dressings, sausages, pork dishes
*Summer savory	18	☐			Flavor egg and bean dishes
‡Sweet marjoram	24		☐		Flavor soups, stews, sausages
†Thyme	6–12	☐	☐		Flavor beef, pork, vegetable dishes

*Annual   ‡Annual in north, Perennial in south
†Perennial   §Biennial

Border Gardens

If you have an expanse of lawn or a group of shrubs, bordering these areas with annuals and perennials can enhance their effect. The border garden is one of the commonest, easiest, and most useful of gardens. Its chief requirements for health and beauty are adequate sun (some fine border plants will thrive in partial shade); a regular program of weeding, staking, and watering during the blooming season; and thorough mulching and fertilizing before winter sets in.

Except in formal gardens, where an effect of primness or severity is an asset, borders should be planted in arcs or curves rather than in straight lines. Even in small plots, do not use specimen (single) plants of one variety. This weakens the impact and tends to give a garden a disorganized look. As I suggested in Chapter Two, orchestrating the color in border gardens is extremely important. If you mix too many hues you may get a rainbow effect that would be pleasing in the sky but is not so on the ground. Plan with care. After choosing the plants you like best for a succession of bloom, consider their colors, their forms, and their heights. Flower forms range from round to spiky. Larkspurs, lupines, and snapdragons are spiky. Round-headed flowers include oriental poppies, peonies, geraniums, and dahlias. Use spire-shaped flowers carefully: too many can disrupt a garden plan, but eliminating them completely leaves a border garden uninteresting and without accent. Play them against round-headed blooms as you would balance a cut arrangement in a vase. It goes without saying that short plants belong in front, tall ones at the back or in the center, but remember that, while some plants remain attractive after their blooming period is over, others (like bleeding hearts) will die and leave a hole that should be masked by other, later-flowering plant material. The quick-growing annuals are very helpful fillers.

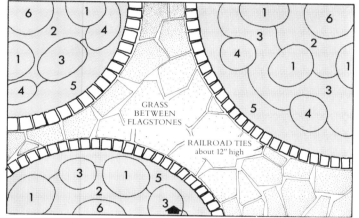

MIDSUMMER BORDER GARDEN

1. Lavender cotton (*Santolina chamaecyparissus*)

2. Gloriosa daisies (*Rudbeckia* 'Orange Bedder')

3. California poppies (*Eschscholzia californica*)

4. Portulaca (*Portulaca grandiflora aurea*)

5. Tickseed, perennial (*Coreopsis grandiflora*)

6. Red-hot pokers (*Kniphofia* 'Primrose Beauty')

Spacing plants requires some knowledge, too, because they all have different growth habits. For effective spacing, remember that the drift, the shape of a group of plants growing naturally, is the best unit of planting to aim for. You can repeat a number of these groups down the length of a border to create an effective design. To make the shapes of your drifts apparent, allow more space between drifts than between the plants within it, and place the flowers relatively close together within the drifts for maximum color effect.

There are hundreds of excellent plants for the border. The lists in Chapter Five and at the back of the book will help you make a custom selection for your own garden beds.

SUMMER-FALL BORDER GARDEN FOR A SOUTHERN CLIMATE

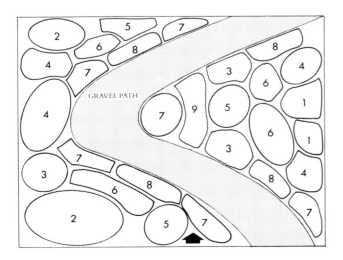

1. Cockscombs (*Celosia argentea plumosa* 'Golden Fleece')

2. Cockscombs (*Celosia argentea plumosa* 'Tango')

3. Cockscombs (*Celosia argentea plumosa* 'Crusader')

4. Canna lilies (*Canna* 'Ambassador')

5. Canna lilies (*Canna* 'Primrose Yellow')

6. Marigolds (*Tagetes erecta* 'Diamond Jubilee')

7. Zinnias (*Zinnia elegans* 'Mini-Pink')

8. Flossflowers (*Ageratum houstonianum* 'Blue Mink')

9. Cockscombs (*Celosia argentea cristata* 'Floradale')

The colors in this border bed are bright, but the gradations are subtle and the effect is unified and soothing.

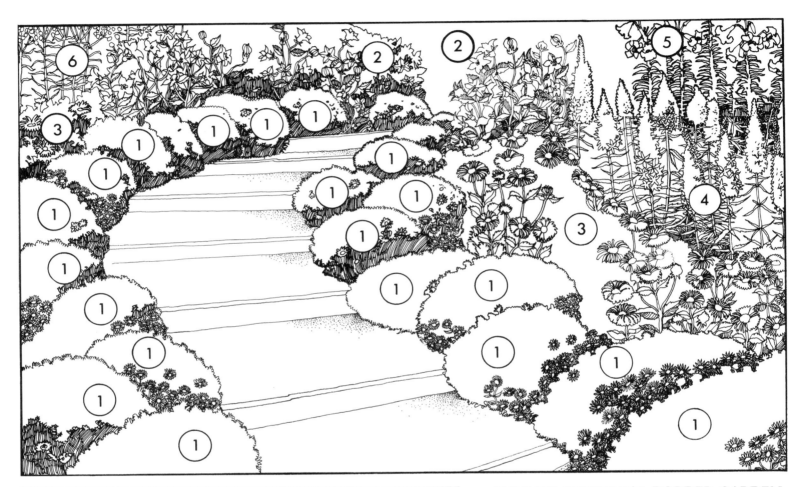

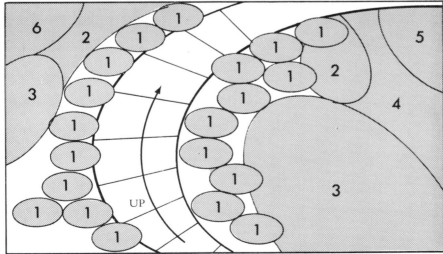

SUMMER PERENNIAL BORDER GARDEN

1. Rock asters (*Callistephus alpinus*)

2. Balloon flowers (*Platycodon grandiflorus*)

3. Orange sunflowers (*Heliopsis scabra incomparabilis*)

4. Loosestrife (*Lythrum virgatum* 'Morden's Pink')

5. Lilies (*Lilium auratum* 'Royal Gold Strain')

6. Baby's breath (*Gypsophila paniculata* 'Perfect')

City Gardens

All kinds of charming, intimate gardens are appearing in our cities, replacing former waste areas. With the new interest in urban gardening have come changes in design ideas and new strains of plants—plants that can withstand polluted air. In San Francisco, Chicago, New York, and many places in between, beautification-of-America and plant-a-tree programs have influenced homeowners. The city garden has become a challenge that offers aesthetic satisfaction and, more important, a pleasant retreat. No matter how small your property, with planning you can create a handsome garden, although the site itself may set limits to the design.

Very informal gardens that imitate nature are almost out of the question, and the urban gardener should avoid putting in too many plants. A simple design is best. By covering much of the garden area with pebbles or with bricks or stones set in pleasing patterns, you can simplify the problem of maintenance. Beds can be small without losing impact if the trees, shrubs, and flowers are chosen and grouped carefully. Raising the beds within wood or stone borders makes an attractive presentation and will improve the soil and drainage. To be fully successful, the garden should also be an extension of the house or apartment, like an outdoor room. The fundamentals of good design, as outlined in Chapter One, apply to the city garden as to any other, and your choices will depend on your preferences, needs, location, and climate.

Gardens on the Ground

Trees and shrubs are the mainstay of any garden, including the small city site. Generally, one large tree is all an urban backyard can accommodate, but two or three smaller trees may be used for balance and scale. They offer shade—protection from the near-desert conditions that often prevail in small paved gardens with light- and heat-reflecting walls. In places where the shade becomes deep, ivy, pachysandra, and ferns will flourish in green peace.

Flowering trees are compact and colorful. They add great beauty and with minimum care they grow well even in adverse conditions. The dogwood is always a good choice, as is the hawthorn, with its white flowers and red berries. The fringe tree seldom grows more than twenty-five feet high and is a mass of white fragrance in spring. The taller sourwood and silk tree are other fine choices, and so are some of the small magnolias.

Fast-growing trees, the deciduous birch and poplar are fine city-garden candidates. Like the ash and Russian olive, they prosper in almost any soil and tolerate neglect. The catalpa is another no-nonsense deciduous tree, and, of course, the very city-hardy ailanthus is always satisfactory, though the flower of the male of the species has an unpleasant smell. The honey locust is also very hardy, and because its foliage is delicate it casts a pleasant light shade. Among the deciduous shrubs, the following are exceptionally resistant to smoke and soot:

Bridal wreath (*Spiraea vanhouttei*)
Dwarf Japanese quince (*Chaenomeles japonica*)
Dwarf sumac (*Rhus copallina*)
Five-leaved aralia (*Acanthopanax sieboldianus*)
Forsythia (many species and hybrids)
Fuzzy deutzia (*Deutzia scabra*)
Japanese barberry (*Berberis thunbergii*)
Peegee hydrangea (*Hydrangea paniculata grandiflora*)
Rose of Sharon (*Hibiscus syriacus*)
Symphoricarpos (most species)
Tatarian honeysuckle (*Lonicera tatarica*)

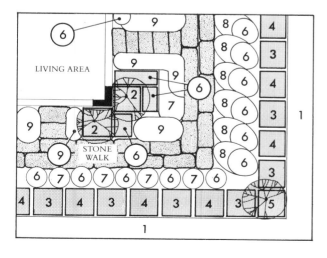

1. European cranberry bushes (*Viburnum opulus nanum*)

2. Hydrangeas (*Hydrangea macrophylla* 'Mariesii')

3. Iris (*Iris ochroleuca gigantea*)

4. Tulips (*Tulipa* 'Inga Hume')

5. Peonies (*Paeonia moutan*)

6. Daffodils (*Narcissus* 'Jeanne d'Arc')

7. Iris (*Iris* 'Lemon Flare')

8. Hyacinths (*Hyacinthus orientalis* 'Lady Derby')

9. Lilies-of-the-valley (*Convallaria majalis*)

Because conifers keep both their color and their shape all winter, an urban garden does well to have some of these evergreen trees and shrubs. Yew is a good selection. A shrub, it lends itself to pruning and has two forms, upright and flat-top. Arborvitae, a popular coniferous tree, is, unfortunately, difficult to grow. Some species burn brown in winter or lose bottom branches. Instead, plant dark-needled hemlocks, fine graceful trees that grow quickly even in the shade. They come in pyramidal, round, and columnar varieties. The pfitzer juniper is robust, has lovely blue-green foliage, and succeeds well in the city. But it does need some sunshine. Dwarf pines and smaller varieties of the Norway spruce are other candidates for city sites.

The conifers need good air circulation, and that is often severely lacking in the city. For this reason it is sometimes more prudent to select broad-leaved evergreens for city gardens, since they can survive in poor conditions. Many varieties tolerate shade, prefer acidity (which is generally characteristic of city soils), withstand soot and smoke to a remarkable degree, have a compact habit of growth, and need little pruning. Northerners should be aware that some plants in this category are evergreen only in the south. Check for this in your nursery catalogue before purchasing.

Rhododendrons (including azaleas) are perhaps the city-dweller's favorite group of evergreen shrubs. There are hundreds of types and colors to choose from. They are spectacular in bloom and remain attractive throughout the year. Consult your local nurseryman, who will know what varieties do best in your area. Most adapt well to city gardens. Some rhododendrons will even bloom in deep shade, whereas azaleas need a little sun. Both kinds, however, must be copiously watered in summer, for they suffer more than most plants if their soil dries out. Several beautiful new varieties of the camellia grow well in shade, bloom yearly, and survive even temperatures close to zero.

Japanese holly, though not as showy as rhododendrons or camellias,

Sweet williams in attractive planters
supply a charming decorative note in
the Burt Getz garden in Phoenix. Who
would pass up the opportunity to sit
and enjoy them?

is a broad-leaved evergreen shrub that tolerates shade and soot and keeps its fine green color. There are many good varieties but some poor ones, so select carefully. Catalogues of reliable nurseries will guide you here. English and American holly (which are trees rather than shrubs but can be contained by shearing) are good choices. The former has dark green, the latter pale green, foliage. Both require some sun. If you want the decorative berries, bed in a male and a female plant relatively close together.

Japanese andromeda is also a good choice. This broad-leaved evergreen produces clusters of white flowers and does well under poor conditions. Species and varieties of the *Berberis* (barberry), *Cotoneaster, Euonymus,* and *Pyracantha* (fire thorn) genera, the holly grape (*Mahonia*), and the Japanese laurel (*Aucuba japonica*) are also rewarding.

You may not have room for a lawn in your backyard, but, whether in small beds or in pots and containers, annual and perennial flowers and bulbs can provide a four-season show. If your garden is enclosed within walls—and most urban gardens are—paint them with vines. Your friends from the country will envy your three-dimensional advantage. Many vines are hardy enough to withstand the most adverse conditions. A list in Chapter Five indicates some of the ones that do best in a city environment.

Gardens in the Air

Rooftop gardening is a challenge because a different set of rules applies and more thought must be given to preparing the site and selecting plants. It is a very ancient art. The Greeks were masters at it. Today, because of overcrowded city conditions, there is a new interest in this kind of gardening. Practically any type of roof can be used: balconies, house or garage rooftops (lush greenery on top of a garage can offer a pretty scene to view from the windows of a two-story house), and apartment or penthouse terraces.

The latter can be costly but they really require no more than a modest outlay and a reasonable amount of planning to be charming.

It may seem possible but is imprudent to unload soil on a roof and just start gardening. Soil must be contained in wooden planters, raised beds, or ornamental pots. Small-container gardening offers many advantages. Plants can be moved about to catch the sun and avoid excess wind, and, in winter, pot plants can do double duty as decoration indoors. Keep in mind that wooden boxes—on casters, if necessary—are easier to move than concrete or stone containers. Structural factors such as weight and drainage must be considered and checked before any boxes or plantings are put in place. It is wise to consult an engineer before proceeding.

Plants in the ground can search for moisture and nutrients deep in the soil, but plants confined to containers need a rich, well-drained topsoil. You should enrich the soil in your larger containers periodically—about once a year. Remove some of the old soil from the boxes—about six inches—and add new soil. Replenishing can be done a little at a time: it need not be done all at once. Like most houseplants, plants in small pots require periodic repotting.

The first step in planning is to select a theme that will unify the landscape. Will the scheme be Japanese, with a few stones and plants? Informal, with considerable freedom of design? Or somewhat formal, with few plants but simple lines? One good scheme, which creates visual variety, is to place planter boxes at various levels, establishing patterns on the floor or against fences or railings.

To make your garden in the air an inviting retreat, use trellises and unusual fence designs to make a place for vines to grow. Vines are excellent for covering an unsightly wall, making a tapestry of green on a trellis, or softening the edge of a planter. There are many wonderful flowering vines, such as clematis and morning glory, and most adapt well to rooftop conditions. Consider a partial ceiling to give a three-dimensional effect and to act as an overhead screen for privacy. A small awning or canopy can also do wonders for a rooftop garden.

Trees and shrubs, annuals and perennials—many plants can be grown on a roof, and since sun is a major asset of many sky-high gardens, do not forget vegetables and herbs. These plants grow beautifully, need no more care than flowers, and offer edible rewards.

Use small trees with picturesque growth habits, like dogwoods or crab apples. Multiple-stem trees are sculptural and break harsh architectural lines. Magnolia and gray birch are two outstanding types. Plantings in the rooftop garden have to withstand severe wind and sun in summer and cold in winter, a good reason to avoid tall, weak-limbed trees. Even with windbreaks, trees may need supplemental wire support: wind can rock trees mercilessly and loosen roots. Use guy wires anchored in deep containers and be sure the portion that goes around the tree is sheathed in a piece of rubber.

Spread mulches—peat moss, fir bark—over earth in containers to prevent rapid drying-out. Your trees and shrubs will need special attention because conditions are always severer in the air than on the ground. A burlap-covered frame or screen will protect plants from freezing or starting their spring growth too early. In early spring, remove all dead wood—small twigs as well as large branches. Limbs rubbing against each other produce wounds in bark through which disease may enter. Trim away all wood broken by high winds.

Moisture is very important in roof gardening. Soil dries out more rapidly than it does on the ground, so slow, deep watering is necessary. Never skimp on water if you want lush plants.

These trees and shrubs will withstand wind better than most plants and are well suited for gardens in the air:

TREES
Cherry (*Prunus*, many species)
Crab apple (*Malus*, many species)
European hornbeam (*Carpinus betulus fastigiata*)
Flowering dogwood (*Cornus florida*)
Ginkgo, or maidenhair tree (*Ginkgo biloba*)
Gray birch (*Betula populifolia*)
Golden-chain tree (*Laburnum watereri vossii*)
Golden-rain tree (*Koelreuteria paniculata*)
Japanese maple (*Acer palmatum*)
Locust (*Robinia*, many species)
Mountain ash, European (*Sorbus aucuparia*)
Norway spruce (*Picea abies*)
Red maple (*Acer rubrum*)
Russian olive (*Elaeagnus angustifolia*)
Scotch pine (*Pinus sylvestris*)
Silk tree, or mimosa (*Albizia julibrissin*)
White pine (*Pinus strobus*)
Willow (*Salix*, many species)

SHRUBS
Cotoneaster (many species)
Euonymus (many species)
Forsythia (many species)
Fire thorn (*Pyracantha coccinea lalandi*)
Glossy abelia (*Abelia grandiflora*)
Holly (*Ilex*, many species)
Japanese andromeda (*Pieris japonica*)
Japanese quince (*Chaenomeles japonica*)
Japanese yew (*Taxus cuspidata*)
Mock orange (*Philadelphus*, many species)
Privet (*Ligustrum*, many species)
Pussy willow (*Salix discolor*)
Rhododendron (many species)
Swiss mountain pine (*Pinus mugo mugo*)

4. FOUR-SEASON GARDENS

A garden is a very personal and intimate thing, revealing the character and habits of the people who tend it. It may be a small city hideaway or a large formal estate. But of whatever kind—whether in the city or the country, as a retreat or a showpiece, moderate in cost or expensive—the four-season garden, filled with color from winter through fall, is the ultimate prize. In the following chapter we look at nine gardens in various parts of the country. None of these gardens was completed in a day or a week or a year; a garden is a growing thing, after all, becoming more beautiful as the years pass, more endearing as the seasons change.

The Richard Scurry Garden,
New York City
SPRING: Colorful tulips and white marguerites bring in the new season, and bursts of green deck the trees. The predominantly white-and-yellow color scheme is both pleasing and subdued, and the arrangement of planters provides a handsome frame for the garden. As the photographs that follow demonstrate, though the plants change as the year advances the charm of this rooftop garden is unfailing.

55

THE RICHARD SCURRY GARDEN, NEW YORK CITY

This penthouse garden, in an area approximately 30 by 40 feet, is **L**-shaped. It has the best of everything—beautiful flowers, handsome trees, perfect dimensions, and decorative planters and furniture. Ideally situated, it commands an impressive view of the Central Park reservoir, and offers privacy because of a brick wall on an adjoining building.

As with most gardens in the air, the owners rely extensively on containers: a few island planters for trees and shrubs and clay pots for plants for additional color in season. The garden is never cluttered or crowded, and the wicker furniture and white and brown containers provide just the right complement to the plants. Color is abundant in spring, with tulips and marguerites. In summer there are marigolds, stocks, and tiger lilies. Fall brings autumnal colors of rust, purple, and gold.

The garden is not only visually delightful but also well planned. The Scurrys have put in two working areas where they can repot and care for the plants. These work centers are especially helpful additions because hauling soil to a terrace garden several times a year is a chore. With places to store soil and pots, work becomes a pleasure.

Because most of the garden is in planters, some replenishing is needed from time to time. The small trees are trimmed occasionally to keep them sculptural—an important task on a roof, where everything must have a balanced look. Other routine care includes proper watering—here a special drip system controlled by an automatic timer that waters plants just enough and not too much. The planters are of concrete and brick and need only an occasional washing to keep them looking handsome.

The brick floor is durable and functional. The pattern is purposely simple, so that it does not detract from furniture and plants. Against the wall of the apartment, contrasting pleasantly with the colorful display of the garden, are statuary and a fish pond. A narrow terrace on the north side, filled with small trees and seasonal pot plants, completes this beautiful four-season garden, an oasis of quiet and beauty.

Rooftop gardens should never be crowded. They work best as colorful retreats from the gray city, and plenty of space should be provided for strolling and sitting. The Scurry garden seems roomy yet lush because plants of a few kinds are displayed neatly in carefully placed containers. Three trees—all crab apples—are just enough to frame the garden and the superb view, and to create a necessary vertical color accent.

Masses of plants are brought in at different seasons to complement those already growing in permanent brick planters. All this rooftop greenery is astonishingly easy to care for. The garden is a place to enjoy, not to toil in—and for urban people, that works well.

SUMMER: In spring this garden was washed with delicate tints of yellow and green (see pages 54–55). Now the color scheme is enriched and deepened as alyssum and marigolds come into bloom; begonias, stocks, and tiger lilies join the colorful display. Trees leaf out, and the garden becomes a joyful summer place.

Fences, screens, and other barriers provide privacy, and rambler roses soften them.

A fine container plant, amaryllis is a welcome floral addition indoors or on a rooftop.

Potted pelargoniums bring brightness to city gardens.

Matthew Barr

Matthew Barr

Matthew Barr

57

Opposite:

FALL: Chrysanthemums massed and distributed through the garden make this autumn scene a memorable one. The plants are deliberately grouped so that each color can speak out boldly. Beautiful natural wicker furniture replaces the white ensemble of summertime, and a highly attractive retreat is the result.

WINTER: Now nature alone is the landscape painter. Snow carpets the ground, dusts the trees, and pillows the furniture. Only the brick planters show color. Bare branches finger a cold sky. Beyond the balustrade stands the city in a gray overcoat.

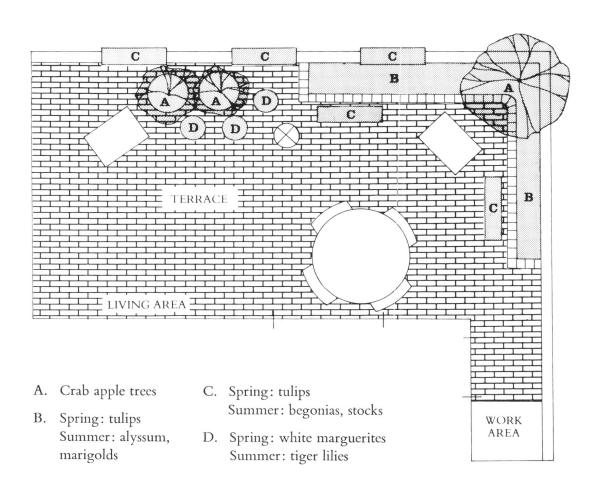

A. Crab apple trees

B. Spring: tulips
Summer: alyssum, marigolds

C. Spring: tulips
Summer: begonias, stocks

D. Spring: white marguerites
Summer: tiger lilies

THE LEOLA B. FRAIM GARDEN, BOSTON

A silky lawn brings serenity to this New England garden. An inviting entrance to the house, it is lined with masses of flowering bulbs in spring and colorful lilies in summer. In fall, the quiet landscape provides solace for the soul. The charming country plan shows European influence, and the garden offers much beauty in return for only a little maintenance.

SPRING: The almond tree at the left bursts into pink flower. Narcissus and daffodils are waking up, and a flowering cherry at the right is a mass of white blossoms. By late spring the garden is in full color.

This charming garden outside Boston, a little larger than an acre, is a fine example of a country garden. It remains visually pleasing all year long—with rare shrubs, velvety lawns, winding paths, and a woodland lot that frames the lovely scene. The owner's husband, a dedicated gardener and a *Hemerocallis* expert, tended the plants for many years, until his recent death. Hundreds of daylilies bordering the fence attest to his enthusiasm.

The informal planting provides interest at almost every turn, and a cohesive plan makes the entire landscape a garden. There are several separate gardening areas, including four perennial borders, a rock garden, a wildflower collection, and a wonderful fernery, where rare plants abound. There is visual delight at all seasons of the year, from the warm days of spring to the gray days of winter, when silhouettes of bare branches create beauty against a snowy background. This is truly a gardener's garden.

Mrs. Fraim's house is screened from the road by masses of rhododendrons, giving the passerby no inkling of what lies behind. In front of the house is a lawn bordered by a galaxy of plantain lilies. Dozens of varieties produce stunning colors and textures—dark leaves with yellow edges and light green leaves with white edges, narrow, broad, and wavy leaves—and many wonderfully fragrant flowers. This border extends to a natural woodland and curves away: here fringed bleeding hearts thrive. Beyond these is a dense ground cover of barrenwort, whose foliage turns bronze in the autumn. Along this woodland edge such perennials as bee balm, spiraea, and trillium grow.

In the shaded woodland, among the glossy ground cover, are rose-colored Japanese primrose and European ginger. Farther off is a massive display of large, clear bluebells.

In the perennial border are viburnums, boxwood bushes, Japanese dogwoods, and a daphne shrub with clusters of white flowers. There is a tree peony with large starlike pods, a tupelo tree for brilliant fall color, a pfitzer juniper, and several varieties of ferns, from bladder fern to maidenhair.

61

Above left:
Yellow alyssum shouts with color, and dwarf purple iris makes a beautiful contrast.

Above right:
Blue forget-me-nots, yellow iris, and Exbury azaleas create a memorable spring scene.

A sophisticated textural effect is achieved with yellow alyssum and white candytuft.

Another garden has heather, daylilies, Solomon's seal, bloodroot, several varieties of trilliums, and red baneberry, with its fernlike leaves and clusters of fuzzy, white blossoms on small spikes.

The rock garden has a white-flowering Judas tree, spring heath, heliotropes, geraniums, and sedums to provide a range of colors and textures, and there is a lovely columbine. Red and white blooms of the lewisia are mixed with the flannel leaves of mullein. The well-known hen-and-chicks fill crevices in the rocks with their sturdy rosettes.

Behind the house, the scene of our feature photographs, is a lush lawn bordered by masses of perennials. One bed contains tree peonies; bright yellow achillea (or yarrow); tansy, with yellow clusters of buttonlike flowers and gray-blue foliage; iris; violet asters; flax; mounds of silver artemisia; and spots of colorful pansies. The alliums (*Allium christophii*, a variety of flowering onion) have lilac flowering heads of almost starlike sheen. Blueberries, marigolds, hydrangeas, and pink spikes of lupine add to the display.

Another bed, set off by an arborvitae hedge and a beautiful sorrel tree, contains an array of perennials: coralbells, lupines, roses, a handsome variety of daylily, and the ground cover Kenilworth ivy (*Cymbalaria muralis*), with its dense mat of leaves and delicate lilac-blue flowers.

A third border perpendicular to the first two has fragrant, purple dame's rocket alongside purple beardtongue and bright orange-yellow spikes of red-hot poker. A variety of daylily ranges from pink and yellow

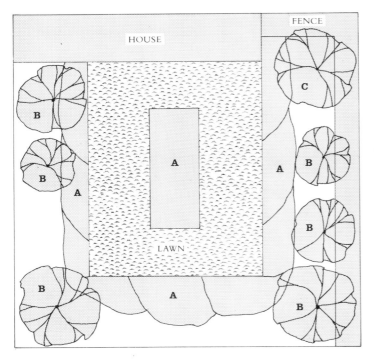

A. Flower beds   B. Flowering trees   C. Evergreen tree

to a lovely peach in early summer, and many more bloom by midsummer. The remaining area has vegetables mixed with thermopsis (false lupines) and more coralbells.

Ornamental shrubs and fragrant trees are strategically placed around these borders. The azaleas start in April, followed by crab apples, viburnums, and snowdrop trees. By late spring the rest of the garden is in bloom with dogwoods and fringe trees. In June the shrub *Stewartia koreana* and a sweet bay tree are in full white bloom, the latter providing a fabulous fragrance. In fall there is Higan cherry with semidouble pink flowers. A hydrangea entirely covers the southwest wing of the house with large flower clusters.

This garden has won several prizes from horticultural societies and is well known in the area, as it should be, because it is a beautiful example of the art of gardening.

Above:
WINTER: The line and form of this rural garden remain even in winter. Bare branches create sculptural drama against the winter sky.

FALL: Flowers are gone, but the garden holds the rich green tones of the luxuriant lawns and abundant plants. All is lush and peaceful.

SUMMER: The advantage of planting one type of flower in masses rather than singly is evident here, where garlands of lilies in several colors are the keynote of summer. Evergreen shrubs in the rear frame the landscape.

66

THE ELDON DANNHAUSEN
GARDEN, CHICAGO

The owner of this garden is a sculptor, and his backyard is a sculptural gem in the heart of a bustling midwestern city. The marriage of concrete-aggregate, water, and plants is also a union of form, texture, and function. A few evergreens, a few deciduous trees provide a frame; rare alpine plants dot the site, and colorful shrubs are also present. Here is reflection, movement, and beauty in a space 25 by 30 feet. Low-growing plants, taller shrubs, and still taller medium-sized trees are placed to give a handsome tiered effect. Rare specimens of bellflowers and wild azaleas, and a weeping beech give the connoisseur's touch to a handsomely honed landscape plan. In the background is the owner's greenhouse, where orchids and bromeliads flourish.

SUMMER: Color bursts forth in summer—yellow daylilies, red geraniums, and white phlox. The bright masses of color are deliberately interrupted with pale orange bellflowers. The ducks on the pond are quite real.

Ambitious city gardens are rare. This one, in a Chicago backyard, is unique. As it happens, I saw it being started twenty-five years ago. It was then a neglected 25-by-30-foot plot overgrown with weeds. A combination of artificial and natural materials was used to create a serene, sylvan setting. Sculptor Eldon Dannhausen's hand is apparent in the design. The textured concrete, poured in curves and arcs, makes a graceful background for rare plants, for Mr. Dannhausen, a dedicated gardener, is an avid plant collector who loves alpine species. In all seasons the garden has something to offer the viewer, and it is always a peaceful, beautiful place to look at and be in.

Many native plants and rock-garden beauties adorn the garden, but always it is the sculptured waterway that steals the show. The pavement patterns are exquisite, reminiscent of ancient Roman gardens, where pavement made as great a statement as the plants. Whether when a study in gray and white in winter, or when ablaze with color in summer, this garden is an outstanding example of what can be done in a small space.

Maintenance is minimal. A weekly cleanup is necessary, as are some pruning of the trees and occasional trimming to keep the plants in sculptural proportion. But otherwise the plants grow pretty much on their own—clear indication of an intelligent plan. There is balance throughout. Instead of large trees, which would dwarf the site, small trees and shrubbery blend together. Since there are no tall trees or shrubs, good periodic pruning and trimming eliminate the need for costly once-a-year pruning.

Most of the garden is composed of wild plants and perennials, so, here again, maintenance is minimal. Perennials perform year after year, of course, but new plants are added now and then because the owner is a collector. If additional color is wanted in summer, seasonal pot plants are set out.

Rocks are rearranged from time to time or new ones put in place, and gravel is replenished when necessary. Rain and an occasional hosing-down keep the pavings shiny and handsome. Because few wild plants can survive in a waterlogged situation, it is imperative that the soil be of the best and that drainage be perfect. Thus, at various times of the year some new soil is added and mulched in place.

Backed by a two-story greenhouse, the Dannhausen garden can be seen from many points of view. It is an oasis, complete with waterway, in the middle of Chicago.

Below left:
The heat of summer dances in the flowers, but the pond at the center of the garden offers cool refreshment for the eye.

Bright yellow and brilliant red lilies make a vivid statement.

Opposite:
FALL: Autumn strokes the garden with shades of gold and red, and although the flowers are almost gone, the garden is very pleasing A handsome European weeping beech stands at the left and rear of the garden, and native azaleas add their color.

Left:
WINTER: The snow-covered mounds stand out like sculpture, and the color scheme of grays, whites, and greens creates a dramatic mood.

Opposite:
SPRING: Trees are coming into leaf: a maple unfolds tiny fingers of red. Evergreens lining the pond and pinkish gray gravel make a handsome combination. The muted colors are effective, and they underline the overall balance, scale, and proportion of the garden.

A beautiful contorted juniper demands attention.

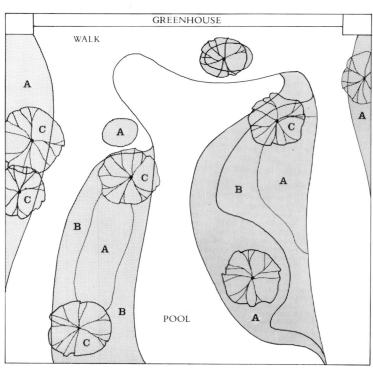

A. Ground cover   B. Perennials   C. Flowering trees

THE WHITNEY STONE GARDEN, CHARLOTTESVILLE

This large garden has been graced by nature for many years, and beauty reigns in all seasons. A handsome, arched wooden gateway and magnificent boxwood bushes frame the view giving on to one of the gardens. Beyond the entrance the eye is greeted by a panoply of colors massed in beds. Hedges define the garden, and, through clever clipping, they are made to echo the shape of the mountain range in the far distance. There is a great deal of color here almost all year. And, though the garden is formal in layout, there are natural touches that enhance its beauty.

SPRING: A plum tree at the entrance bursts into blossom as warm weather starts, but the climbing rose on the arbor is still a garland of green. Tulips shout with color, and the view from the vantage point of the gate is breathtaking. Notice that the tulips are arranged in masses of one color and that color carries the eye to the manicured boxwood hedges in the far distance.

This grand garden, called Morven, was started in the 1890s. The present owners bought the property in 1926 and through a careful restoration program, which lasted three years and required the assistance of a landscape architect, they returned the garden to good condition. Almost three acres, Morven was originally a spring and fall retreat for the owners, so color is bountiful at these times of the year. However, even in summer and winter there is abundant beauty.

The total garden is made up of several gardens, some formal, some for cutting. Like European gardens of the early 1900s, it also has a conservatory. Though the terrain is flat, the landscape is so well planned that there is both balance and variety throughout. The formality of the garden lies mostly in its charming walls and hedges of elegant boxwood and euonymus, which give a feeling of intimacy to a rather large area.

The garden relies heavily on such spring-flowering bulbs as daffodils and tulips (8,000 are planted each year), but there are also many shrubs, with azaleas in profusion and lovely crab apples resplendent in their season.

The flower beds are laid out in regular patterns, yet because of the backdrop of trees the effect is not austere. On the contrary, with its picket fences, gates, and other country accents, this is a garden to be at home in.

Because it is large, Morven requires professional care, but in a garden so long established, many of the usual chores are eliminated. For example, old trees and shrubs almost care for themselves, and good turf does the same. Routine bedding of seasonal plants is of course necessary, and so is a good deal of trimming and pruning. Periodic clipping of both trees and shrubs maintains the lines of the overall plan.

Annuals, perennials, and bulbs are replaced as needed with fresh plantings each year. New soil is added and beds revitalized when necessary. Azaleas dot the property and, though these require little care, proper acid feeding must be done.

75

The clever arrangement of beds creates unusual, unexpected beauty at every time of year—one always seems to be looking down long corridors of rich green perfectly accented with colorful sequences of flowers. A wooden pergola and several white gates also provide visual variety.

During the last week of April, Morven is open to the public to enjoy.

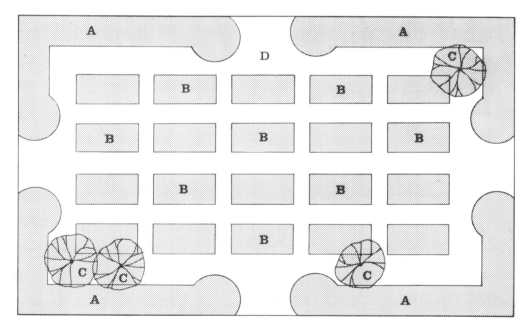

TULIP GARDEN

A. Evergreen hedge

B. Tulip beds

C. Flowering trees

D. Lawn

Tulips make exquisite mosaics of color against the green lawn.

Left:
A handsome rustic pergola beckons at the end of a path.

Below left:
FALL: Rich green now predominates in lawns and hedges. Chrysanthemums and asters announce the season.

Below right:
WINTER: Magnificent columnlike evergreens frame the entrance to the flower garden, where smaller globe-shaped boxwood bushes stand like sentries, waiting for spring. Beds are mulched and ready for the color on its way.

Opposite:
SUMMER: The tulips are gone now, but in their place are enough perennials to please any gardener. There are pink and red painted daisies, shasta daisies, phlox, salvias, rock cress, and speed-wells.

THE WILLIAM NATHANIEL
BANKS GARDEN, ATLANTA

This vast flowerland, well known and beautifully landscaped, is composed of many gardens. We feature here the lovely border garden that lines the main area, and, in our late winter shot, the beds on the other side of the wall. Lining the ivy-covered brick walls there are abundant flowers, brimming over the paths to create a buoyant feeling. The border garden is separated from the more formal bedding areas, where masses of flowers are grown in season. Judicious selection of plants produces a tapestry of color, with occasional vibrant hues for drama. There is never a dull moment in this traditional garden.

FALL: In spring and summer the border is mixed in color; in autumn chrysanthemums spill forth, masses of white and yellow as far as the eye can see. On the right, providing a perfect accent, are red roses, their deep tint echoed softly by a scattering of pink chrysanthemums.

The original design of the grounds, by landscape architect William C. Pauley, dates back to 1929. In this elegant country garden, where long walks and paths provide spatial interest, color abounds in almost all seasons. It covers 300 acres, but the organization has logic and cohesion. As you walk from one area to the next you can anticipate what lies ahead; the garden's beauty is startling, but it unfolds in a thoroughly plausible way.

Much of the estate is woodland (oaks, pines, poplars). There are five major garden areas: a lawn and lake; a formal flower garden; a fountain garden; a pool and bath pavilion; and a boxwood garden with gazebo. In addition, there are a number of less formal areas: a small azalea "room," a camellia walk, and a cutting garden.

The great wedge-shaped, shrubbery-bordered *tapis vert*, framed by old trees, sweeps down from the house to the landscape's focal point, a ten-acre lake, whose cool beauty is echoed elsewhere on the property by several fountains and a lily pool.

The formal flower garden is surrounded by an ivy-covered brick wall. Along this wall runs a magnificent border bed, and, since the changes of season are most evident here, we have chosen to feature it in our spring, summer, and fall photographs; however, the whole garden is resplendent with blossoms from late March through October, beginning with thousands of daffodils to welcome spring. Five of the thirteen center beds are in floribunda roses, five in peonies, and three in begonias. In early spring there are red and yellow tulips and, all over the place, azaleas, pink and white dogwoods, and blossoming fruit trees. In early May the roses and peonies bloom, and, in the borders, there are foxgloves, early daisies, Dutch iris, sweet williams, and violas. In summer comes the perennial white phlox; marigolds and pink and white zinnias replace the bulbs; and flossflowers replace the violas. There are also astilbes, Stokes' asters, and clumps of yellow daylilies in the borders. Spectacular pink spider plants (*Cleome spinosa*) bloom all summer. In the fall, chrysanthemums (yellow, pink, and

white) replace the annuals. New bulbs—several thousand of them—are planted in November or December to bloom the following spring.

The fountain garden has borders of boxwood bushes and plantings of pink and white tulips (Mariette and White Triumphator, the lily-flowered type). Pink and white impatiens replace the tulips in summer. The Carrara marble fountain was carved in Italy in the 1840s for an estate in north Georgia. Its three tiers of lion masks and dolphins spout water.

The swimming pool is surrounded by a hedge of Fosteri holly backed by photinia and crape myrtle. The pool house, or pavilion, is Venetian in style, with pineapple finials and a striped canopy roof. Fruit trees bloom in the boxwood garden in spring: white peach, Hopa crab, Kwanzan cherry, and pink and white dogwood. The boxwood, which is of the slow-growing English variety, was planted more than forty years ago. The owner's father moved it from a cousin's place where it had been growing for about fifty years—so the plants are almost a century old.

There are ancient white oaks and pines. Wild azaleas, honeysuckle, and many varieties of camellias bloom in the woods. There are peacocks and, on the lake, ducks, geese, and swans.

A multitude of bordered walks provides total retreat from the world. There are few private gardens so well planned and maintained as this one. It is vast, and it is truly a masterpiece.

WINTER: Spring is not far behind. Daffodils are flags of color in their mulched beds, contrasting with the dark green ivy that covers the wall.

Opposite:
SPRING: Here next to the wall, white shasta daisies and foxgloves bloom in the back, with blue violas in the front of the bed bordering the brick path. Note the perspective of the border and how the line carries the eye to the greenery beyond. The ivy on the brick walls provides a perfect foil for the flowers.

SUMMER : In summer presents a totally
different picture against the handsome
brick-and-ivy backdrop, with white
phlox, marigolds, and pink zinnias.

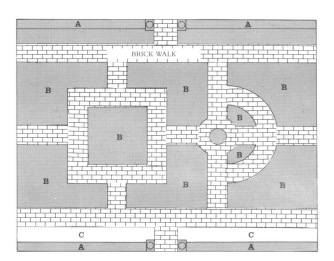

BRICK WALK

FORMAL FLOWER GARDEN

A. Ivy-covered wall

B. Flower beds

C. Perennial border

Pink and white wax begonias carpet a
bed in profusion.

Opposite:
Roses provide a dainty contrast
exuberant cleomes.

A beautiful viburnum droops gracefully
over the emerald lawn.

Seldom are cleomes so handsomely
displayed.

THE BURT GETZ GARDEN, PHOENIX

Swimming-pool gardens can sometimes be bleak—but not this one. A small area, blazing with the colors of seasonal pot plants, is enlarged by a beautiful backdrop of mountains and palms. The stark white walls offer effective contrast. Because the climate is warm, the spring and summer scenes are much the same, for flowers last through both seasons. Maintenance is minimal. This is a true oasis in the desert, where flower color is intense and very welcome.

WINTER: This may look like a summer scene, but it is winter that is pictured here. Pink geraniums and white petunias flow over one wall, and there are more pink petunias in the background and in pots.

Arizona is blazing hot in summer, and a garden in this state is indeed an oasis. The Getzes' swimming-pool garden—part of a larger garden on about an acre—is brilliant with color almost all year. The magic here is in the seasonal pot plants, chiefly petunias and chrysanthemums, brought in to augment the scene. This excellent example of a container garden beautifully fulfills its intended purpose—to provide color in the desert. The containers are chosen with care and are planted with masses of flowers, not just a few. In the height of summer, however, the pool garden is cool and lush because green is a dominant color. Another feature of the plan is the series of walls at varying levels, which creates an interesting terraced effect. Neither formal nor informal, this pool garden is very contemporary.

In addition to the swimming-pool garden there are rose gardens on the property, and an immense orchard of citrus trees provides a backdrop for the entire scene. Off the kitchen there are vegetable and herb gardens. The transitions from one garden to another are sophisticated and smooth.

The other side of the wall is just as pretty as the pool garden, and the rich green of citrus and palm trees lends welcome coolness to the poolside view. Violas spill out of pots on the terrace.

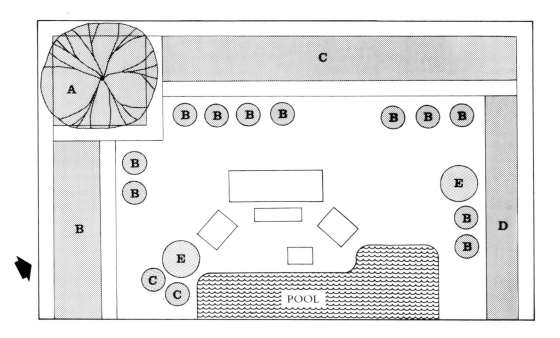

SPRING–SUMMER: Colorful petunias continue to bloom, along with brilliant geraniums and masses of lavender flowers against the far wall. The colors are vibrant but controlled.

Opposite:
FALL: Geraniums still supply color in fall, but now chrysanthemums of many hues add an autumnal note. White and yellow mums line one wall, brilliant against a lush green backdrop.

90

THE J. GORDON DOUGLAS GARDEN, SANTA BARBARA

It would be hard to find a more attractive entrance to a home than this terraced garden. Throughout, there is a sensible proportion. The tall evergreens at the rear are a backdrop for the annuals and perennials that blaze with beauty almost all year long. Gravel walks provide detail, and a sculptured bird bath makes a central focal point. The placement of the plants gives a feeling of depth, and the intensity of color, especially evident in summer and fall, is a delight.

SUMMER: The colorful marguerites in the foreground steal the show in summer, but the roses also demand attention. Marigolds add a dramatic note of gold to the red and pink garden. Altogether, there is a great wealth of color throughout the season.

Here, white candytuft makes a carpet of snow over a warm stone wall.

Though this six-acre garden was started in 1923, it can be called old-fashioned, or Victorian. Miss Jorck of Beverly Hills did the original landscaping, which has been changed very little. The present owners are both avid horticulturists, and they share their garden every spring with groups of students from various universities.

There is color here at all times of the year, and in the Santa Barbara climate, where the weather is constant, the seasonal change in the plants is very welcome. It is the perennials that supply all-year beauty.

The name of the Douglas estate, Il Brolino, means "fenced in by hedges" in Italian, and there are a multitude of these. Also in the Italian manner are the large statues, urns, and balustrades. The house, too, reflects classic Mediterranean design.

The entrance is a sixteen-foot iron gate, arched in the center and flanked by two high pilasters, each topped with a carved Italian urn. The driveway, made of large, thick stones, has an Italian look. Straight ahead, past the house, a second, similar, gateway leads to the lower gardens, where a long vista ends in a tall Italian pottery urn standing on a four-foot base. Ivy geraniums flow down its sides.

The cutting garden qualifies as both a viewing and a working garden and it supplies the family with vegetables as well as flowers of many kinds, including an abundance of roses. There are flowers to be cut for the house in all seasons of the year.

At the front of the house some steps and terraces lead to one of the main features of Il Brolino: a magnificent topiary garden, where shrubs are sculpted into the shapes of animals and birds. Above the topiary garden is another terrace with terra-cotta balustrades enclosing white tree oleanders, a fountain, and two magnolias. Between and slightly behind the magnolia trees is a large stone structure, which holds a life-size statue of Diana of the Hunt. Close by stands the largest eucalyptus tree in southern California, shaped and towering like a mighty flower. In the far background, ridged mountains complete the picture.

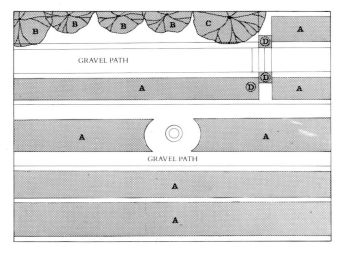

TERRACE GARDEN

A. Flower beds

B. Evergreens

C. Citrus

D. Evergreen shrubs

WINTER: This garden is just as colorful in winter as in summer. Here white candytuft is in full glory, and white and purple nicotiana add their beauty in the foreground. There are poppies, asters, and flossflowers, and a notable eucalyptus stands sentry behind.

Opposite:
FALL: Now the beauty of white azaleas and roses, with masses of white and yellow chrysanthemums at the rear, provides a refreshing change. This is an exceptionally colorful all-season garden.

To the right of the main topiary garden is a smaller one, the "bridge-card garden," where hedges and flowers outline the borders and centers of four large playing cards—the aces of clubs, diamonds, hearts, and spades. To the left is an evergreen garden consisting of four boxwood beds, each with a flowering pear tree at its center. An extensive drip system irrigates plants and hedges, conserving much water. There is a fountain in the middle of the walk.

Next comes a rose garden, and on the other side a flagstone path leads to a Japanese garden, which has a pond with a small stone bridge. The area is planted with many types of ferns, azaleas, iris, primroses, hydrangeas, and spring bulbs, and there are tall Monterey pines to provide shade.

Beyond the Japanese garden, to the west and north, are a few massive live oaks shadowing a glade of a thousand clivia plants. Beyond the clivias are several hundred lilies-of-the-Nile, whose lush beauty reminds one of Claude Monet's gardens in Giverny.

To the east of the house, and partly framed by it, is a walled patio garden with a lawn in the center. The wall is covered with night-blooming jasmine and climbing roses.

To the west of the house, down some stone steps, is the sunken Italian garden. It has high stone walls on two sides and a balustrade on another. In the center is a large well raised on three octagonal steps. Carved from a single piece of stone, the well was imported from Florence, as was the statuary.

Farther to the west, through an ornamental wrought-iron gate and up three stone steps, is a small stone garden house with an 1894 cornerstone (the building is now a State of California Historical Landmark). To the south is a small court looking out over the sea toward the Channel Islands. Still farther west is the swimming pool, bordered by large stone planters and a flower bed.

Below the pool and a small lawn, stone steps descend to the rose garden and six flower beds, each a hundred feet long, at different levels.

SPRING: Spring brings masses of yellow marguerites to full bloom; above them are petunias and, still farther along the terrace, roses. At the rear of the garden, near the stone steps, are white azaleas and yellow and orange zinnias.

The pattern and texture of this scene are beautifully handled.

Opposite:
This exquisite topiary garden was planned to contrast elegantly with the flower gardens.

From the terrace on the south side of the house, a stone stairway leads to a long flagstone walk flanked by English ivy borders and surrounded by lovely lawns. This walk leads in turn to an oval flagstone terrace with a balustrade, bordered with camellias. At its center is a magnificent live oak, beautifully trimmed and manicured.

Below this terrace and to the south is another lawn, this one with a rectangular lily pond. In back are giant Monterey pines.

At the back of the house, to the east, is an arched breezeway and courtyard. Below and to the south is a long vegetable garden arranged in terraces and flanked by two gravel walks. There is a large lemon orchard farther to the southwest.

THE MILO SCOTT BERGESON GARDEN, SAN FRANCISCO

This small rooftop garden is beautiful in all seasons. The key accent is the handsome white filigree gazebo, a perfect foil for colorful flowers, useful in summer as a shady nook. The garden is filled with evergreen shrubs for all-year interest and attractive topiaries and standards for drama. Seasonal pot plants offer vibrant color, and there is ample seating in this city retreat. The Bergesons' charming green world flourishes with minimal maintenance.

Opposite:
FALL: Cascading chrysanthemums announce the fall season, and white chrysanthemums in pots provide a perfect complement to them. The topiaries stay rich and green through all seasons. The effect is lush and inviting.

A fine bonsai maple provides an attractive accent.

This townhouse roof garden is a showplace, well decorated with plants, and a restful retreat from city crowds for its owners. It requires little maintenance but provides many hours of enjoyment. The design is purposely modest, not only to permit easy upkeep but to give a feeling of intimacy and charm. There are no hills or valleys or ancient trees to support the landscape, and no wild growth to work with. The garden was planned carefully and relies on planter boxes and fences to create its effect.

San Francisco is a city of one season (the climate is almost always moderate in temperature), but the owners wanted a seasonal garden. Their effort succeeds in reflecting the progression of colors that might take place if the weather changed. Camellias and azaleas are the backbone. Fuchsias also figure in the basic arrangement. Against these perennial plants, annuals act as decorative touches, and, though it may appear that a great deal of work is involved in caring for the garden, each "change of season" requires only about a week's work.

A 20-by-30-foot rectangle, the Bergesons' garden could have been monotonous, but it is not. They installed a decorative center of interest—the handsome scroll gazebo—which gives the space dimension and visual interest. And it also provides the shade-loving plants with the darker surroundings they thrive in.

Small gardens need small plants, so here there are no masses of large trees or shrubs. Instead, the Bergesons grow well-trained standards (plants trained to grow with a single short stem and a crown of foliage) and topiaries for year-round color, augmenting them with seasonal flowering plants grown in pots. The sculpted plants show an artist's hand, an artist who understands the need for a calm and orderly look.

The floor is covered with handsome concrete aggregate and a grid pattern of wood rails for interest. Hosing down the floor takes but a few minutes. The glass fences framed in wood allow light to enter yet provide protection from the wind, and they repeat the grid pattern of the floor.

101

Opposite:

WINTER: Poinsettias take center stage around the gazebo and provide stellar winter color—contrasting with the evergreen shrubs. Azaleas are just beginning to show some color, and the camellias in the foreground and bamboo at the right provide leafy beauty.

SPRING: Now the camellias and pots of pink azaleas are flanked with masses of white marguerites. White azalea standards bloom, one on each side of the gazebo, and the handsome topiaries in small pots add decorative outline and greenery.

The handsome boxwood topiaries are well trained and beautifully grown.

Another topiary, another delightful accent.

Masses of hydrangeas make a powerful statement in this small garden.

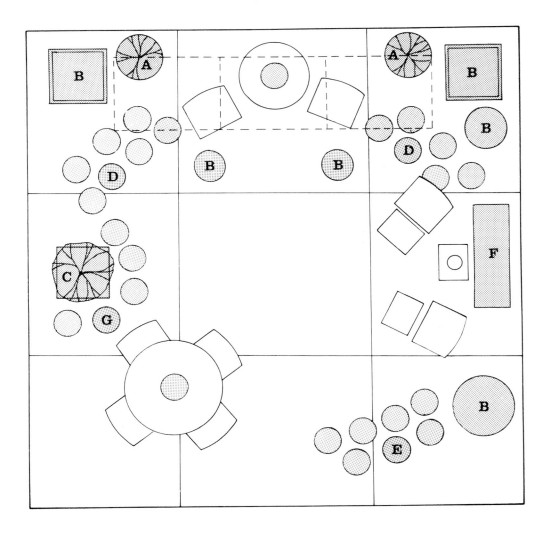

SUMMER GARDEN

A. Trees

B. Evergreen shrubs

C. Evergreen tree

D. Hydrangeas

E. Fuchsias

F. Marigolds

G. Annuals

This is a container garden, and the planters and boxes, which are important components in its working, require some special care. The Bergesons repot their small perennial plants from time to time and enrich the soil in the large containers. They also set out annuals like impatiens and pot marigolds at the proper seasonal time.

Because there are no exceptionally delicate plants here, this garden can provide its panorama of beauty with a minimum of watering and feeding, and of course the handsome topiaries, which stay rich and green through the seasons, need little care.

Because of its symmetry, this rooftop garden can be called formal, though there are enough accents in the way of containers to create a mixed style. Color is used with an artist's touch; there are no shocking or jarring notes; the color schemes are well thought out for every season. Altogether, this is a garden to live in and enjoy.

THE MRS. CORYDON WAGNER GARDEN, TACOMA

In this spectacular garden the beds are set handsomely against a blue pool. The lawn and brick walk make a perfect marriage of texture and pattern. The frame of the garden is a stand of tall Douglas firs, which also provide a fine vertical accent in a somewhat horizontal garden plan, and in front of the firs are rows of shrubs. The design is tiered from the boxwood around the beds, to shrubs, to trees, and thus a satisfying sense of dimension is achieved throughout. There is continual interest here, and the colorful beds of flowers are subtle and yet effective in color. It would be hard to find a more excellent garden—surely a garden for all seasons.

Opposite:
Seen at close range, the spring garden dissolves into flurries of white and pink.

This handsome garden, which covers ten acres, is one of the finest examples of landscape architecture in the northwestern United States. Designed by Thomas Church, it is a collection of several gardens, and the layout—a bit formal, a bit natural—owes something to both the Repton style of Victorian times and the Robinson and Jekyll style of the early 1900s. Although the property is vast, each garden makes its own statement, and there is a cohesiveness in the total design that validates the garden's reputation.

The garden consists basically of evergreens, tall deciduous trees, and flowering shrubs, but abundant flowers fill in the framework, making each season a visual delight. Spring, summer, fall, and winter evoke very different moods. The herb and topiary gardens are charming, and beyond the

A. Evergreens

B. Flowering trees

C. Flowering shrubs

D. Flower beds

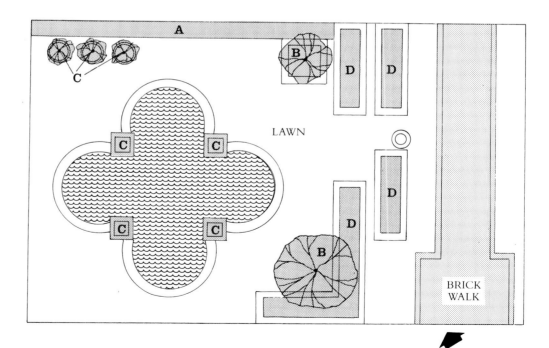

Opposite:
SPRING: Spring bursts forth with a flurry, and the flowering fruit trees are masses of blooms. There are magnificent beds of tulips, azaleas in containers, and a horse chestnut tree behind them.

The narrow palette of colors in this fine herb garden is subtle and pleasing. Here is a masterful exercise in the handling of texture and form.

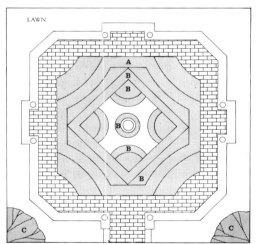

HERB GARDEN

A. Boxwood hedge

B. Herbs

C. Flowering trees

Left:
WINTER: Handsome lawns and manicured boxwood hedges create a peaceful winter landscape. The pool at the rear adds a striking blue accent. Notice how the various textures of brick, lawn, and plants provide visual interest.

Below left:
SUMMER: A rainbow of zinnias, marigolds, cosmos, and snapdragons replaces the tulips. The green canopies of flowering trees and shrubs support the floral display.

Opposite:
FALL: Autumn foliage takes over in the background, beautifully complemented by massed chrysanthemums. White petunias and colorful vincas complete the picture.

main gardens there are great expanses of rare roses and beautiful rhodo-dendrons.

This Tacoma garden relies on the strength and durability of venerable trees and shrubs and the richness of a magnificent lawn. Its elements—including the fine boxwood hedges, so beautifully maintained—seem to demand a great deal of care, but they really do not. True, seasonal plantings must be made, and clipping and pruning require some time. Beds are prepared and fresh soil is added yearly to keep plants vigorous. Masses of tulips are put in the ground every third year, annuals are replenished yearly, perennials need division and staking. But these are all pleasant, not arduous, tasks. The lawns are fed, watered, weeded, or revitalized according to the season, but here again the task is merely routine because a well-established lawn needs no exceptional efforts of maintenance.

On this beautifully planned estate, man and nature work together at their best. Obviously such beauty was not created overnight. The present owners have treasured this garden for more than twenty years. It is a large part of their lives, and they clearly enjoy sharing its richness with others, for many garden clubs tour the grounds each year. ·

5. THE DESIGN POTENTIAL OF PLANTS

Trees and Shrubs

Structure is the basic consideration in the four-season garden, and trees, shrubs, and flowers are the elements. Begin by establishing a framework of carefully selected trees and shrubs. Plant them as soon as your master plan is on paper. They will grow while you work on other areas of your garden.

The tree as a design element is a vertical accent, almost an exclamation point. A few such verticals are fine—too many, and the garden is doomed. Trees must be used with restraint or the result will be busy, unsettling. The most important factor in selecting trees is proportion. The size of the trees must be in proportion to the size of the whole garden. In general, the average garden—of, say, 60 by 100 feet—can comfortably accommodate only four trees. The gardener may decide on one large tree to dominate the whole area, or two or three smaller trees, or three or four medium-to-very-small trees. Balance and proportion are the keys here: four large trees would dwarf everything else, four small trees might look puny. A mixture of trees of not too different sizes is usually the best choice.

When choosing a tree, consider the other elements it will interact with: your house, the portion of property it will fill and cover with shade when mature, and the heights of other trees and shrubs nearby.

Too large a tree will dominate a house and make it look insignificant, so, if you have a small house, it is best to select small trees. If your house is low and horizontal, tall, columnar plantings around it will give it an awkward, caged appearance. Shorter round or vase-shaped plants will give a more graceful, expansive look.

When choosing trees for your garden, think also of their canopy diameter. Spreading trees give much shade. Be sure to plant them where you want it. If these trees are placed too close together, their branches may intertwine, inhibiting balanced growth and blocking the sun from the plants and grass below. If your property includes two or three trees with overlapping canopies, it might be wise to remove one. Nonspreading trees give little shade and can be planted close together to make a screen or windbreak.

Like trees, shrubs come in many shapes and sizes. Do not hesitate to use them to achieve the effects you want. A low, spreading type can make a high wall look lower. Tall, erect ones placed at the corners of your house will soften the harsh vertical lines yet emphasize the importance of the building in the total landscape. Plant shrubs in groups of two or three, three or five, five or seven, and so on, depending upon size. Avoid using one kind of shrub and then, set apart by itself, another kind. Group the plants for maximum effect, and do not be afraid to let the branches interlace. This creates a woven-tapestry effect that is very pleasing.

Shrubs also have very individual textures. A shrub that has large leaves creates a coarse-textured effect, while one with small leaves appears fine-textured. It is the texture that we see from a distance. When selecting shrubs, combine textures to create the rhythm so often lacking in gardens. Like color, textures have advancing and receding qualities. By placing a small quantity of the largest texture in front and a large quantity of the finest texture behind, a shallow area can be made to seem deeper.

Trees and shrubs can be categorized according to the kind of foliage they have: coniferous evergreen, broad-leaved evergreen, and deciduous. The evergreens offer year-round color. The needle-bearing or coniferous type, which includes the spruces, firs, cedars, and pines, are bushy, heavy-textured, and sculptural. Conifers always appear darker than other plants because their foliage absorbs a great deal of light. Too many create an almost sepulchral effect. The pattern of the foliage is pronounced, a factor that should also be considered when you select them for your garden. Their cones make a decorative contribution to the winter scene.

Broad-leaved evergreen foliage is generally large and glossy, and it admits and reflects a good deal of light. Unlike the conifers, which tend to screen and shelter, broad-leaved evergreens like the rhododendrons and hollies can open up a garden plan. The broad-leaved evergreen shrubs are popular because many of them not only retain their foliage color through the year but bloom as well.

Deciduous plants—those that drop their leaves in fall—are as important in any garden plan as evergreens. They bring a soft emerald backdrop to the garden in spring and summer and a blaze of yellows, reds, oranges, and purples to the scene in the fall—then their silhouettes become the bone structure of the landscape in winter.

In selecting deciduous trees, consider not only summer shade and autumn color but also the line pattern the bare branches will make against a frosty sky. Each deciduous tree has a definite crown shape—upright, horizontal, or pendant. (An oak, for example, has upward-sweeping branches, a dogwood's limbs are horizontal, a weeping beech has a drooping silhouette.) Keep in mind also that the young tree you select at the nursery looks quite different from the mature tree it will become in a few years.

Shrubs can be placed near deciduous trees to extend or emphasize a line. At the corner of a tall house a tree-and-shrub group with arching branches will tie the vertical line into the horizontal line of the ground. The lighter structures of deciduous shrubs are indispensable in the garden. In the cold-climate garden they will predominate. Their soft green foliage makes a perfect foil for the herbaceous plants of summer, but they must be used in the same manner as deciduous trees because their branches will be bare in winter.

Many of the broad-leaved evergreen and deciduous shrubs, and some deciduous trees as well, flower at certain seasons of the year. These highly ornamental plants are versatile. Use them as accents or mass them against a wall or fence. Placed at the back of a bed, they work in harmonious partnership with the annual and perennial flowers in front. They come in a whole spectrum of colors, and their sequence of bloom ranges from the beginning to the end of the growing season.

Some Excellent Deciduous Trees for Special Regions

Tree	Conspicuous Flowers	East	North	Great Plains	West	Lower Pacific Coast	South	Lower South
Ash, green (*Fraxinus pennsylvanica lanceolata*)			☐	☐				
Ash, modesto (*Fraxinus velutina glabra*)					☐	☐		
Ash, white (*Fraxinus americana*)		☐		☐			☐	
Bauhinia	☐					☐	☐	☐
Beech, European (*Fagus sylvatica*)		☐		☐	☐			
Beech, purple (*Fagus sylvatica atropunicea*)		☐				☐		
Birch, cutleaf weeping (*Betula pendula gracilis*)				☐	☐	☐		
Birch, paper (*Betula papyrifera*)		☐	☐	☐				
Box elder (*Acer negundo*)		☐	☐	☐	☐			
Buttonwood, or sycamore (*Platanus occidentalis*)		☐	☐		☐	☐	☐	
Catalpa (*Catalpa speciosa*)						☐	☐	
Cherry, flowering (*Prunus serrulata*)	☐	☐		☐	☐	☐	☐	
Coral tree (*Erythrina americana*)	☐						☐	☐
Cottonwood (*Populus deltoides*)				☐	☐			
Crab apple (*Malus*)	☐	☐		☐	☐	☐	☐	
Dogwood (*Cornus*)	☐	☐			☐	☐	☐	

Tree	Conspicuous Flowers	East	North	Great Plains	West	Lower Pacific Coast	South	Lower South
Elm, Chinese (*Ulmus parvifolia*)						☐	☐	
Elm, Siberian (*Ulmus pumila*)		☐	☐	☐				
Frangipani (*Plumeria rubra*)	☐							☐
Ginkgo, or maidenhair tree (*Ginkgo biloba*)		☐		☐	☐	☐	☐	
Golden-chain tree (*Laburnum watereri*)	☐	☐			☐	☐		
Golden-rain tree (*Koelreuteria paniculata*)	☐	☐			☐	☐	☐	
Hawthorn (*Crataegus*)	☐	☐		☐	☐	☐	☐	
Honey locust, common (*Gleditsia triacanthos*)		☐		☐	☐		☐	
Honey locust, moraine						☐		
Horse chestnut, common (*Aesculus hippocastanum*)	☐	☐	☐		☐	☐		
Linden, American (*Tilia americana*)		☐	☐	☐	☐			
Linden, small-leaved European (*Tilia cordata*)		☐	☐	☐				
Maple, Amur (*Acer ginnala*)		☐	☐					
Maple, Norway (*Acer platanoides*)		☐	☐					
Maple, red (*Acer rubrum*)		☐	☐	☐	☐			
Maple, vine (*Acer circinatum*)					☐			

Tree	Conspicuous Flowers	East	North	Great Plains	West	Lower Pacific Coast	South	Lower South
Oak, pin (*Quercus palustris*)		☐			☐		☐	
Oak, red (*Quercus rubra*)		☐		☐	☐			
Oak, willow (*Quercus phellos*)							☐	
Pea tree (*Caragana arborescens*)	☐	☐		☐				
Redbud, or judas tree (*Cercis canadensis*)	☐	☐		☐	☐	☐	☐	
Royal poinciana (*Delonix regia*)	☐							☐
Russian olive (*Elaeagnus angustifolia*)		☐	☐	☐	☐	☐		
Silk tree, or mimosa (*Albizia julibrissin*)	☐	☐				☐	☐	☐
Silver-bell tree (*Halesia carolina*)	☐	☐				☐		
Stewartia (*Stewartia koreana*)	☐	☐						
Sweet gum (*Liquidambar styraciflua*)		☐		☐	☐	☐	☐	
Tulip tree (*Liriodendron tulipifera*)	☐	☐			☐		☐	
Tupelo, or pepperidge, or sour gum (*Nyssa sylvatica*)		☐		☐		☐	☐	
Walnut, black (*Juglans nigra*)		☐		☐			☐	
Walnut, English (*Juglans regia*)					☐	☐		

Trees for Shade and Show

Tree	Zone	Type	Conspicuous Flowers	Height	Use
African tulip tree (*Spathodea campanulata*)	9	broad-leaved evergreen	scarlet—summer	large	background, specimen
Alder, black (*Alnus glutinosa*)	4	deciduous		large	background, specimen
Alder, Italian (*Alnus cordata*)	5	deciduous		large	specimen
Arborvitae, American; or white cedar (*Thuja occidentalis*)	3	coniferous evergreen		medium	specimen, windscreen
Ash, flowering (*Fraxinus ornus*)	6	deciduous	white—spring	medium	background, framing, specimen
Ash, green (*Fraxinus pennsylvanica lanceolata*)	2	deciduous		large	background, specimen, windscreen
Ash, white (*Fraxinus americana*)	4	deciduous		large	background, framing
Bald cypress (*Taxodium destichum*)	4	deciduous		large	background, specimen
Beech, American (*Fagus grandifolia*)	4	deciduous		medium	background, shade, specimen
Beech, European (*Fagus sylvatica*)	5	deciduous		large	background, shade, specimen
Beech, purple (*Fagus sylvatica atropunicea*)	5	deciduous		large	background, shade, specimen
Birch, cutleaf weeping (*Betula pendula gracilis*)	2	deciduous		medium	specimen (handsome pendant habit)
Birch, gray (*Betula populifolia*)	4	deciduous		medium	background, framing, specimen
Birch, paper (*Betula papyrifera*)	2	deciduous		large	background, framing, specimen

NOTE: "Zone" indicates the coldest region in which a plant can survive (see the Temperature Zone Map on page 168).
Trees grow to different heights in different areas: "small" indicates to 20 feet, "medium" indicates to 50 feet, "large" indicates over 50 feet.

Tree	Zone	Type	Conspicuous Flowers	Height	Use
Buttonwood, or sycamore (*Platanus occidentalis*)	5	deciduous		large	background, shade
Catalpa (*Catalpa speciosa*)	5	deciduous	white—summer	large	background
Cedar, atlas (*Cedrus atlantica*)	6	coniferous evergreen		large	background, specimen
Cedar, deodar (*Cedrus deodara*)	7	coniferous evergreen		large	background, specimen
Cedar of Lebanon (*Cedrus libani*)	5	coniferous evergreen		large	background, specimen
Cherry, flowering (*Prunus serrulata*, many varieties)	6	deciduous	pink, rose, white—spring	medium	background, framing, specimen
Cherry, rosebud (*Prunus subhirtella*)	4	deciduous	pink—spring, fall	medium	specimen
Coral tree (*Erythrina americana*)	9	deciduous	scarlet—summer	small	background, specimen
Cork tree (*Phellodendron chinense*)	3	deciduous		large	background, specimen
Crab apple (*Malus*, many species and varieties)	varies	deciduous	white, pink—spring	small, medium	background, framing, specimen
Dogwood, flowering (*Cornus florida*)	5	deciduous	pink, white—spring	small	background, specimen
Dogwood, Japanese (*Cornus kousa*)	5	deciduous	white—spring	small	background, specimen
Douglas fir (*Pseudotsuga menziesi*)	4	coniferous evergreen		large	background, windscreen
Eastern red cedar (*Juniperus virginiana*)	3	coniferous evergreen		large	background, specimen, windscreen
Elm, American (*Ulmus americana*)	2	deciduous		large	background, specimen

121

Tree	Zone	Type	Conspicuous Flowers	Height	Use
Elm, smooth-leaved (*Ulmus carpinifolia*)	5	deciduous		large	background, specimen
Fir, white (*Abies concolor*)	4	coniferous evergreen		large	background
Frangipani (*Plumeria rubra*)	10	deciduous	pink, purple, white	small	framing, specimen
Fringe tree (*Chionanthus virginicus*)	5	deciduous	white—spring	medium	specimen
Ginkgo, or maidenhair tree (*Ginkgo biloba*)	5	deciduous		large	background, framing, specimen
Golden-chain tree (*Laburnum watereri*)	6	deciduous	yellow—spring	medium	background, framing, specimen
Golden-rain tree (*Koelreuteria paniculata*)	6	deciduous	yellow—summer	small	background, specimen
Hawthorn (*Crataegus,* many species and hybrids)	5	deciduous	white, pink red—spring	medium	background, specimen
Hemlock, Canadian (*Tsuga canadensis*)	3	coniferous evergreen		medium	background, hedge, windscreen
Hickory (*Carya ovata*)	5	deciduous		large	background, specimen
Holly, American (*Ilex opaca*)	6	broad-leaved evergreen		medium	framing, specimen
Holly, English (*Ilex aquifolium*)	6	broad-leaved evergreen		medium	framing, specimen
Honey locust, common (*Gleditsia triacanthos*)	4	deciduous		large	background
Hornbeam, European (*Carpinus betulus*)	6	deciduous		medium	hedge, windscreen
Horse chestnut, common (*Aesculus hippocastanum*)	3	deciduous	white—spring	large	background, framing, shade, specimen

Tree	Zone	Type	Conspicuous Flowers	Height	Use
Japanese cedar (*Cryptomeria japonica*)	7	coniferous evergreen		large	background, specimen
Japanese pagoda tree (*Sophora japonica*)	5	deciduous	white—summer	medium	specimen
Judas tree (*see* Redbud)					
Juniper, Chinese (*Juniperus chinensis*)	4	coniferous evergreen		medium	specimen
Larch, European (*Larix decidua*)	2	deciduous		large	background
Larch, Japanese (*Larix kaempferi*)	5	deciduous		large	specimen, windscreen
Linden, American (*Tilia americana*)	2	deciduous		large	background, shade
Linden, small-leaved European (*Tilia cordata*)	4	deciduous		large	background, shade, specimen
Locust, black (*Robinia pseudo-acacia*)	5	deciduous	white—spring	large	background, specimen
London plane tree, or plane tree (*Platanus acerifolia*)	5	deciduous		large	background, shade
Magnolia, saucer (*Magnolia soulangiana*)	6	deciduous	white-purple—spring	medium	specimen
Magnolia, southern (*Magnolia grandiflora*)	7	broad-leaved evergreen	white—spring-summer	large	background, specimen
Maple, Amur (*Acer ginnala*)	2	deciduous		medium	framing, hedge, specimen, windscreen
Maple, Japanese (*Acer palmatum*)	5	deciduous		medium	specimen
Maple, Norway (*Acer platanoides*)	3	deciduous		large	background, shade

Tree	Zone	Type	Conspicuous Flowers	Height	Use
Maple, red (*Acer rubrum*)	4	deciduous		large	background, shade, specimen
Maple, sugar (*Acer saccharum*)	3	deciduous		large	background, shade, specimen
Mimosa (*see* Silk tree)					
Mountain ash, European (*Sorbus aucuparia*)	3	deciduous	white—spring	medium	background, framing, specimen
Oak, cork (*Quercus suber*)	7	broad-leaved evergreen		large	specimen
Oak, holly (*Quercus ilex*)	9	broad-leaved evergreen		large	specimen
Oak, live (*Quercus virginiana*)	7	broad-leaved evergreen		large	shade, specimen
Oak, pin (*Quercus palustris*)	5	deciduous		large	background, specimen
Oak, red (*Quercus rubra*)	5	deciduous		large	background
Oak, scarlet (*Quercus coccinea*)	5	deciduous		large	shade, specimen
Oak, white (*Quercus alba*)	4	deciduous		large	background, specimen
Pea tree (*Caragana arborescens*)	4	deciduous	yellow—spring	small	specimen, windscreen
Peach, flowering (*Prunus persica*, many varieties)	5	deciduous	pink, red—spring	medium	specimen
Pear, Bradford ornamental (*Pyrus calleryana Bradford*)	5	deciduous	white—spring	medium	framing, specimen
Pecan (*Carya illinoensis*)	6	deciduous		large	specimen
Pepperidge (*see* Tupelo)					

Tree	Zone	Type	Conspicuous Flowers	Height	Use
Pine, Austrian (*Pinus nigra*)	4	coniferous evergreen		large	specimen, windscreen
Pine, Monterey (*Pinus radiata*)	7	coniferous evergreen		medium	specimen
Pine, ponderosa (*Pinus ponderosa*)	4	coniferous evergreen		large	background, specimen
Pine, red (*Pinus resinosa*)	3	coniferous evergreen		large	specimen, windscreen
Pine, Scotch (*Pinus sylvestris*)	3	coniferous evergreen		large	background, specimen
Pine, white (*Pinus strobus*)	3	coniferous evergreen		large	background, specimen
Plane tree (*see* London plane tree)					
Redbud, or judas tree (*Cercis canadensis*)	5	deciduous	purple—spring	medium	background, specimen
Royal poinciana (*Delonix regia*)	9	deciduous	scarlet—summer	medium	specimen
Russian olive (*Elaeagnus angustifolia*)	3	deciduous		small	specimen, windscreen
Serviceberry, shadblow (*Amelanchier canadensis*)	4	deciduous	white—spring	medium	background, specimen
Shaving-brush tree (*Pachira aquatica*)	10	deciduous		large	background, specimen
Silk tree, or mimosa (*Albizia julibrissin*)	7	deciduous	yellow-pink—summer	medium	background, specimen
Silver-bell tree (*Halesia carolina*)	5	deciduous	white—early spring	small	background, specimen
Sorrel tree (*see* Sourwood)					
Sour gum (*see* Tupelo)					

125

Tree	Zone	Type	Conspicuous Flowers	Height	Use
Sourwood, or sorrel tree (*Oxydendrum arboreum*)	5	deciduous	white—summer	medium	background
Spruce, Colorado blue (*Picea pungens*)	3	coniferous evergreen		large	background, specimen
Spruce, Norway (*Picea abies*)	3	coniferous evergreen		large	background, windscreen
Spruce, white (*Picea glauca*)	2	coniferous evergreen		large	background, specimen, windscreen
Stewartia (*Stewartia koreana*)	5	deciduous	white—summer	small	framing, specimen
Sweet gum (*Liquidambar styraciflua*)	5	deciduous		large	background, framing, shade, specimen
Sycamore (*see* Buttonwood)					
Tulip tree (*Liriodendron tulipifera*)	5	deciduous	greenish white— spring	large	background, framing
Tupelo, or pepperidge, or sour gum (*Nyssa sylvatica*)	4	deciduous		large	background, specimen
Walnut, black (*Juglans nigra*)	5	deciduous		large	background, framing, specimen
Walnut, English (*Juglans regia*)	6	deciduous		large	specimen
Western red cedar (*Juniperus scopulorum*)	5	coniferous evergreen		medium	background, specimen
White cedar (*see* Arborvitae, American)					
Willow, weeping (*Salix babylonica*)	6	deciduous		medium	specimen

A Checklist of Popular Shrubs

DECIDUOUS

Shrub	Zone	Conspicuous Flowers	Berries, Fruit	Height	Use
Azalea (*Rhododendron*, many species and hybrids)	4	many colors— spring, summer		low, medium	shrub border
Barberry, Japanese (*Berberis thunbergii*)	4	yellow—spring	red	medium	shrub border
Beauty bush (*Kolkwitzia amabilis*)	5	pink—spring		tall	background, shrub border
Bellflower, or enkianthus (*Enkianthus*)					
E. campanulatus	5	cream-pink— spring		tall	background, shrub border
E. perulatus	5	white—spring		medium	shrub border
Broom (*Cytisus*)					
C. kewensis	6	white, yellow— spring		low	rock garden, shrub border
C. nigricans	6	yellow—summer		medium	shrub border
Butterfly bush (*Buddleia*)					
B. alternifolia	5	many colors— summer		tall	background
B. davidii	5	blue, lilac— summer		medium	background, shrub border
Cinquefoil, shrubby (*Potentilla fruticosa*)	2	yellow, white— summer, fall		medium	accent, shrub border
Cornelian cherry (*Cornus mas*)	5	yellow—spring	red	tall	accent, shrub border

NOTE: "Zone" indicates the coldest region in which a plant can survive (see the Temperature Zone Map on page 168).
Shrubs grow to different heights in different areas: "low" indicates to 3 feet, "medium" indicates to 5 feet, "tall" indicates to 15 feet.

Shrub	Zone	Conspicuous Flowers	Berries, Fruit	Height	Use
Cotoneaster					
C. acutifolius	3	pink—spring	black	tall	background, hedge, shrub border
C. apiculatus	5	red—spring	orange-red	medium	background, shrub border
C. divaricatus	5	pink—spring	red	medium	background, shrub border
C. horizontalis	5 (semievergreen in warmer areas)	pink—late spring	red	low	shrub border
C. integerrimus	3	pink—spring	red	medium	background, shrub border
Crape myrtle (*Lagerstroemia indica*)	7	many colors—late summer, fall		tall	accent, background, shrub border
Daphne, february (*Daphne mezereum*)	5	lilac, pink—spring	red	medium	background, shrub border
Deutzia					
D. gracilis	5	white—spring		medium	background, shrub border
D. parviflora	5	white-purple—spring		medium	background, shrub border
Dogwood (*Cornus*)					
C. alternifolia	3	white—late spring	blue	tall	accent, background, shrub border
C. racemosa	3	white—spring	white	medium	accent, background, shrub border
C. sericea	3	white—spring	bluish white	medium	background, shrub border
Euonymus, winged; or winged spindle tree (*Euonymus alata*)	4	yellow—spring	red	tall	background, shrub border

128

Shrub	Zone	Conspicuous Flowers	Berries, Fruit	Height	Use
Forsythia (many species and hybrids)	5	yellow—spring		low, medium	accent, background, shrub border
Hibiscus, or rose of Sharon (*Hibiscus syriacus*)	5	many colors—late summer, fall		tall	accent, background, shrub border
Honeysuckle (*Lonicera*)					
L. *fragrantissima*	5	white—spring	red	tall	background
L. *tatarica*	3	many colors— spring	red, yellow	tall	background
Hydrangea					
H. *arborescens grandiflora*	5	white—summer, early fall		medium	background, shrub border
H. *macrophylla*	7	blue, pink, white— summer, early fall		tall	background, shrub border
H. *paniculata grandiflora*	4	white, turning pink— summer, early fall		tall	background, shrub border
Jasmine, winter (*Jasminum nudiflorum*)	5	yellow—late winter, early spring		tall	background, shrub border
Lilac (*Syringa*, many species and hybrids)	3	many colors—spring		tall	accent, background, shrub border
Mock orange (*Philadelphus*, many species and hybrids)	5	white—summer		medium, tall	background, shrub border
Privet, California (*Ligustrum ovalifolium*)	6 (semievergreen in warmer areas)	white—summer	black	tall	background, hedge, shrub border
Privet, common (*Ligustrum vulgare*)	5	white—summer	black	tall	background, hedge, shrub border
Pussy willow (*Salix discolor*)	2	gray catkins— spring		tall	background, hedge

Shrub	Zone	Conspicuous Flowers	Berries, Fruit	Height	Use
Quince (*Chaenomeles*)					
C. cathayensis	5	many colors—spring	yellow-green	tall	accent, background, shrub border
C. japonica	5	reddish orange—spring	yellow	medium	shrub border
C. japonica alpina	5	white—spring	yellow	low	shrub border
Rose (*Rosa*, many species and hybrids)	3	many colors—spring, summer, fall	red, orange, black	medium	accent, shrub border
Spiraea					
S. albiflora	5	white—summer		low	shrub border
S. bumalda	5	white, pink—summer		low	shrub border
S. prunifolia	5	white—spring		medium	accent, background, shrub border
S. thunbergii	5	white—early spring		medium	accent, background, shrub border
S. vanhouttei	5	white—spring		medium	accent, background, shrub border
Summer sweet (*Clethra alnifolia*)	4	white, pink—late summer, fall		tall	background
Tamarisk (*Tamarix*)	5	pink—late summer, early fall		tall	background
T. hispida	7	pink—late summer, fall		medium	background
T. ramosissima	5	pink—late summer, early fall		tall	background
Viburnum (many species and hybrids)	varies	white—spring, summer, fall	black, blue, red	medium, tall	background, shrub border

Shrub	Zone	Conspicuous Flowers	Berries, Fruit	Height	Use
Weigela (many species and hybrids)	varies	many colors— late spring		medium	background, shrub border
Witch hazel (*Hamamelis*)					
H. mollis	5	yellow—early spring		tall	background
H. vernalis	6	yellow—late winter, early spring		medium	shrub border
H. virginiana	5	yellow—late fall		tall	background

EVERGREEN

Shrub	Type	Zone	Conspicuous Flowers	Berries, Fruit	Height	Use
Abelia, glossy (*Abelia grandiflora*)	broad-leaved	6	pink—summer, fall		medium	background, hedge, shrub border
Allamanda, bush (*A. neriifolia*)	broad-leaved	9	deep yellow—summer		medium	background, shrub border
Andromeda (*Pieris*)						
P. floribunda	broad-leaved	5	white—spring		medium	shrub border
P. japonica	broad-leaved	6	white—spring		medium	accent, background, shrub border
Azalea (*Rhododendron*, many species and hybrids)	broad-leaved	4	many colors—spring, summer		low, medium	shrub border
Barberry (*Berberis*)						
B. darwinii	broad-leaved	7	reddish yellow—spring	purple	medium	accent, background, hedge, shrub border
B. julianae	broad-leaved	5	yellow—spring	blue-black	medium	hedge, shrub border
B. mentorensis	broad-leaved	5	yellow—spring	red	medium	shrub border
Bog rosemary (*Andromeda polifolia*)	broad-leaved	4	white—spring		low	rock garden
Boxwood (*Buxus*)						
B. microphylla	broad-leaved	6			low	border, hedge
B. microphylla koreana	broad-leaved	5			low	border, hedge
Camellia (many species and hybrids)	broad-leaved	6	many colors—early spring, spring, fall, winter		medium	accent, background, shrub border
Cotoneaster						
C. horizontalis	semievergreen in zones 8–10 only (see deciduous shrub checklist)					

Shrub	Type	Zone	Conspicuous Flowers	Berries, Fruit	Height	Use
C. microphyllus	broad-leaved	7	white—summer	red	low	rock garden, shrub border
Daphne						
D. cneorum	broad-leaved	5	pink—spring, fall	yellow, then black	low	hedge, rock garden, shrub border
D. odora	broad-leaved	5	purple-red—early spring		medium	hedge, shrub border
Euonymus, Japanese (*Euonymus japonica*)	broad-leaved	7	greenish white—spring	pink-orange	tall	background, shrub border
Fire thorn (*Pyracantha*)						
P. atalantioides	broad-leaved	7	white—spring	orange-red	tall	accent, background, shrub border
P. coccinea	broad-leaved	6	white—spring	orange-red	medium	accent, shrub border
Heath (*Erica*)						
E. darleyensis	broad-leaved	6	pink—late fall, winter		low	edging, rock garden, shrub border
E. tetralix	broad-leaved	4	rose—summer, fall		low	edging, rock garden, shrub border
Hibiscus, Chinese (*Hibiscus rosa-sinensis*)	broad-leaved	9	many colors—spring, summer, fall		tall	accent, background, shrub border
Holly (*Ilex*)						
I. cornuta	broad-leaved	7		red	tall	accent, background, hedge, shrub border
I. crenata	broad-leaved	6		black	tall	accent, background, shrub border
Holly grape (*Mahonia*)						
M. aquifolium	broad-leaved	5	yellow—spring	blue	low	shrub border
M. repens	broad-leaved	5	yellow—spring	black	low	shrub border

Shrub	Type	Zone	Conspicuous Flowers	Berries, Fruit	Height	Use
Japanese laurel (*Aucuba japonica*)	broad-leaved	8		red	low	accent, shrub border
Juniper (*Juniperus*, many species and hybrids)	coniferous	4			low, medium	accent, hedge, shrub border
Mountain laurel (*Kalmia latifolia*)	broad-leaved	4	pink, white— summer		medium	accent, background, shrub border
Oleander, common (*Nerium oleander*)	broad-leaved	8	many colors— spring, summer		tall	accent, background, hedge, shrub border
Osmanthus						
O. delavayi	broad-leaved	7	white—spring		medium	shrub border
O. heterophyllus	broad-leaved	6	white—summer		medium	accent, background, hedge, shrub border
Pine, dwarf white (*Pinus strobus nana*)	coniferous	3			medium	shrub border
Pine, Swiss mountain (*Pinus mugo*)	coniferous	4			low, tall	hedge, shrub border
Privet (*Ligustrum*)						
L. japonicum	broad-leaved	7	white—summer		tall	background, hedge, shrub border
L. ovalifolium	semievergreen in zones 8–10 only (see deciduous shrub checklist)					
Rhododendron (many species and hybrids)	broad-leaved	4	many colors—spring, summer		medium, tall	accent, background, shrub border
Skimmia						
S. japonica	broad-leaved	8	white—spring	red	medium	shrub border
S. reevesiana	broad-leaved	9	white—spring	red	low	shrub border

Shrub	Type	Zone	Conspicuous Flowers	Berries, Fruit	Height	Use
Viburnum (many species and hybrids)	broad-leaved	5	white, pink— spring, summer	black, blue, red	medium, tall	background, shrub border
Yew (*Taxus*)						
T. baccata repandens	coniferous	6		brown	low	hedge
T. cuspidata	coniferous	5		scarlet	tall	hedge

Annuals, Biennials, and Perennials

Annuals, which grow from seed to flower in one season, are particularly valuable in the midsummer garden, when spring bulbs are waning and fall-blooming plants are gaining strength. Some come early: stocks and snapdragons are popular in spring before perennials hit their stride. Some linger late: China asters and zinnias planted in July can carry color well beyond most fall perennials.

Annuals are versatile. You can use them in massed plantings for a high-impact effect or sow them like a ribbon along a path, or as a boundary between areas. They are wonderful edging plants and pinch-hit like veterans in bare spots and places where quick color is needed. They flourish in containers and hanging baskets, and any extra pots of annuals you plant will serve as understudies for shrubs and perennials that fail or become temperamental.

Most annuals prefer a sunny location but there are some that do well in shade or partial shade. For those often troublesome or uninteresting spots begonias, butterfly flowers, foxgloves, impatiens (balsam), sweet alyssum, and vincas (periwinkles) are particularly useful.

Slow-developing types like vervain, petunias, sweet williams, and snapdragons benefit by an early start. They should either be sown in boxes indoors in early spring or purchased in flats from a nursery. Other annuals —including the ever-popular nasturtiums, marigolds, and cosmos—grow quickly and easily in the ground. The proper time to start them from seed depends upon the last date of frost in your area, and this information is given on seed packets. Prestarted plants can go into your garden as soon as the trees are in leaf and the soil is warm.

Annuals are more delicate than perennials and require more frequent watering, shallow cultivation, and occasional light feeding.

ANNUAL GARDEN

1. Zinnias (*Zinnia elegans* 'Snow Time')

2. Marigolds (*Tagetes erecta* 'Diamond Jubilee')

3. Sweet alyssum (*Lobularia maritima* 'Carpet of Snow')

4. Wax begonias (*Begonia semperflorens cultorum* 'Viva')

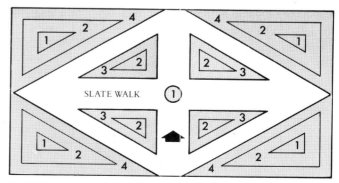

Biennials bloom twice and then die. You can sow seed in the late summer or fall and overwinter the seedlings in a coldframe or in the garden if you mulch them carefully for frost protection. Most of your favorite biennials can be purchased as plants and treated like annuals.

Perennials are hardy and dependable, and few gardens can be without them. They bloom from year to year, reproduce themselves and, once planted, almost care for themselves. Use them to distribute color through the seasons and from one part of the garden to another. Remember, though, that they will not all be in full bloom at the same time. Some perennials offer profuse bloom in early summer and fall, some in spring. Many of the early plants bloom again in late fall—delphiniums and leopard's bane, for example.

Even in a border of exclusively perennial plants, with careful planning and transplanting it is quite possible to conceal bare spots where one type of plant has passed its season. The very useful annual and perennial foliage plants fill such unsightly gaps and make an attractive foil for surrounding flowers. You might choose the annual burning bush (*Kochia scoparia tricophylla*), coleus, dusty miller (*Centaurea* and *Cineraria* species), and snow-on-the-mountain (*Euphorbia marginata*), and the perennial artemisia and lamb's ears (*Stachys lanata*).

When you plan a perennial border, you will generally put the tallest plants behind shorter ones and the smallest in front, but it is often pleasant to bring a mass of tall plants up to the edge to avoid monotony. A background of shrubs or a hedge brings out the beauty of flowers, but remember to leave at least two feet between bed and shrubbery to avoid competition between plants.

Like the annuals, there are perennials for shade. Some of the most popular are: astilbes, bleeding hearts, bugloss, Christmas and Lenten roses, lilies-of-the-valley, lobelias, plantain lilies, primroses, and Virginia bluebells.

138

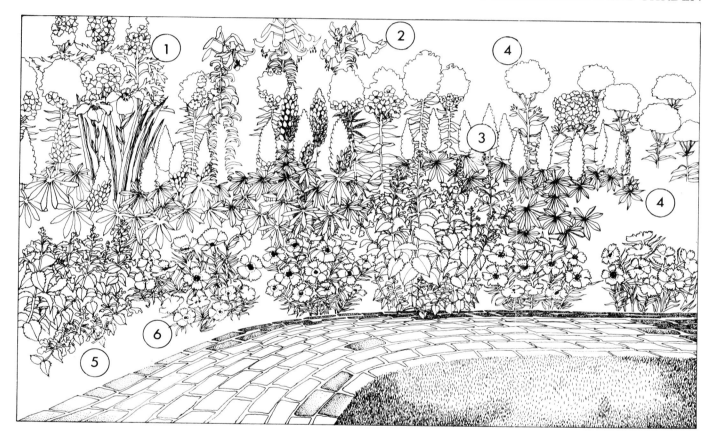

1. Delphiniums (*Delphinium* 'Bellamosum')

2. Lilies (*Lilium*, Aurelian hybrid)

3. Lupines (*Lupinus*, Russell hybrid)

4. Phlox, garden (*Phlox paniculata*)

5. Catmint (*Nepeta mussinii*)

6. Pinks (*Dianthus* 'Zing')

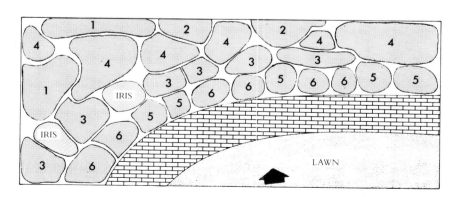

Flowers for Every Season

ANNUAL & BIENNIAL

Flower	Position	Height	Season	Colors
Acroclinium (*Helipterum manglesii*)	sun	12–24 inches	summer to frost	beige, pink, white
African daisy (*Arctotis*)	sun	24 inches	summer to frost	mixed
Ageratum (*see* Flossflower)				
Baby's breath (*Gypsophila elegans*)	sun	15–24 inches	spring, summer	pink, white
Bachelor's button, or cornflower (*Centaurea cyanus*)	sun	12–36 inches	spring, summer	blue, pink, purple, white
Balsam (*see* Impatiens)				
Begonia, wax (*Begonia semperflorens cultorum*)	sun, shade	5–10 inches	spring to frost	pink, red, white
Blanket flower, or gaillardia (*Gaillardia pulchella*)	sun	12–20 inches	summer to frost	cream, red, yellow, mixed
Browallia	sun, some shade	8–18 inches	summer	blue, violet, white
Butterfly flower (*Schizanthus*)	sun, some shade	18–24 inches	summer	various
California poppy (*Eschscholzia californica*)	sun	12–24 inches	spring to frost	orange, pink, red, yellow
Calliopsis (*see* Tickseed)				
Candytuft, common (*Iberis umbellata*)	sun, some shade	8–30 inches	spring, summer	pink, purple, red, white
Candytuft, rocket (*Iberis amara*)	sun, some shade	4–30 inches	spring or fall	pink, purple, red, white
Canterbury bells (*Campanula medium*)	sun	10–36 inches	spring, early summer	blue, pink, purple, white

NOTE: This list includes plants commonly treated as annuals or biennials.

Flower	Position	Height	Season	Colors
Cape marigold (*Dimorphotheca pluvialis*)	sun	12–24 inches	summer	orange, white, yellow, mixed
Carnation (*Dianthus caryophyllus*)	sun	12–24 inches	summer	red, white, yellow, mixed
China aster (*Callistephus chinensis*)	sun, some shade	6–30 inches	summer to frost	various
Chrysanthemum (several species and hybrids)	sun	24–48 inches	summer to frost	various
Clarkia	sun, some shade	24–36 inches	summer	pink, purple, red, white
Cockscomb (*Celosia argentea*)	sun	18–24 inches	summer to frost	orange, pink, red
Convolvulus (*see* Dwarf morning glory)				
Cornflower (*see* Bachelor's button)				
Cosmos	sun, some shade	4–10 feet	summer	pink, red, white
Dahlia	sun	15–60 inches	summer to frost	various
Dwarf morning glory, or convolvulus (*Convolvulus tricolor*)	sun	12 inches	spring, summer	various
English daisy (*Bellis perennis*)	sun	4–8 inches	spring, summer	pink, purple, red, white
Farewell-to-spring, or godetia (*Godetia amoena*)	sun, some shade	12–30 inches	summer	various
Flossflower, or ageratum (*Ageratum houstonianum*)	sun, some shade	6 inches (some to 24 inches)	summer	blue, pink, white

Flower	Position	Height	Season	Colors
Forget-me-not (*Myosotis sylvatica*)	sun, some shade	8–24 inches	spring	blue, pink, white
Four o'clock (*Mirabilis jalapa*)	sun	18–36 inches	summer to frost	various
Foxglove (*Digitalis purpurea*)	shade	24–60 inches	spring, summer	various
Gaillardia (*see* Blanket flower)				
Geranium, or pelargonium (*Pelargonium*)	sun, some shade	4–60 inches	summer to frost	pink, red, white
Globe amaranth (*Gomphrena globosa*)	sun	12–18 inches	summer	pink, red, white
Godetia (*see* Farewell-to-spring)				
Heliotrope (*Heliotropium*)	sun	12–24 inches	summer	blue, lilac
Hollyhock (*Althaea rosea*)	sun	24–60 inches	summer	various
Impatiens, or balsam (*Impatiens balsamina*)	sun, shade	24–30 inches	summer	various
Lantana	sun	18–36 inches	summer to frost	various
Larkspur (*Consolida ambigua*)	sun, some shade	12–48 inches	spring, summer	blue, pink, purple, white
Lobelia, edging (*Lobelia erinus*)	sun, some shade	2–6 inches	spring, summer	blue, pink, white
Love-in-a-mist, or nigella (*Nigella damascena*)	sun	12–18 inches	summer	blue, pink, purple, white
Lupine (*Lupinus hartwegii*)	sun, some shade	12–36 inches	summer	blue, pink, white

142

Flower	Position	Height	Season	Colors
Marigold (*Tagetes erecta*)	sun	8–40 inches	summer to frost	bronze, orange, yellow
Mignonette (*Reseda odorata*)	sun, some shade	6–18 inches	summer	red, white, yellow
Morning glory (*Ipomoea purpurea*)	sun, some shade	15–20 feet (climbs)	summer	various
Nasturtium (*Tropaeolum*)	sun	12–18 inches (climbers to 10 feet)	summer to frost	various
Nemesia	sun	8–18 inches	summer	various
Nicotiana	sun, some shade	12–36 inches	summer	various
Nigella (*see* Love-in-a-mist)				
Painted tongue (*Salpiglossis sinuata*)	sun	15–36 inches	summer	various
Pansy (*Viola wittrockiana*)	sun, some shade	4–8 inches	spring, summer, fall	various
Pelargonium (*see* Geranium)				
Periwinkle (*see* Vinca)				
Petunia	sun, some shade	12–24 inches	summer	various
Phlox (*Phlox drummondii*)	sun, some shade	8–18 inches	spring, summer	various
Pincushion flower (*Scabiosa*)	sun	14–36 inches	summer to frost	blue, pink, purple, white
Pink (*Dianthus*)	sun	8–24 inches	spring, summer	pink, purple, red, white
Poppy, Shirley (*Papaver rhoeas*)	sun	12–36 inches	summer	orange, pink, red, white

Flower	Position	Height	Season	Colors
Portulaca, or rose moss, or sun moss (*Portulaca grandiflora*)	sun	2–8 inches	summer	various
Pot marigold (*Calendula officinalis*)	sun	12–24 inches	summer to frost	cream, orange, yellow
Rose moss (*see* Portulaca)				
Salpiglossis (*see* Painted tongue)				
Salvia, or scarlet sage (*Salvia splendens*)	sun, some shade	15–36 inches	summer to frost	red
Scabiosa (*see* Pincushion flower)				
Scarlet sage (*see* Salvia)				
Snapdragon (*Antirrhinum*)	sun	6–36 inches	spring, summer	various
Spider plant (*Cleome spinosa*)	sun, shade	36–60 inches	summer to frost	pink, white
Stock (*Matthiola*)	sun, some shade	12–30 inches	spring	various
Strawflower (*Helichrysum bracteatum*)	sun	12–30 inches	summer	pink, red, white, yellow, mixed
Sunflower (*Helianthus*)	sun	2–10 feet	summer	brown, orange, yellow, mixed
Sun moss (*see* Portulaca)				
Sunrays (*Helipterum roseum*)	sun	18–24 inches	summer to frost	pink, red, white, yellow

Flower	Position	Height	Season	Colors
Sweet alyssum (*Lobularia maritima*)	sun, some shade	3–8 inches	spring to frost	pink, purple, white
Sweet pea (*Lathyrus odoratus*)	sun, some shade	15–36 inches (climbers more)	spring, summer	various
Sweet william (*Dianthus barbatus*)	sun	4–24 inches	summer	pink, red, white
Tickseed, or calliopsis (*Coreopsis*)	sun, some shade	12–36 inches	spring, summer	brown, orange, red, yellow, mixed
Torenia (*see* Wishbone flower)				
Vervain (*Verbena*)	sun	6–15 inches	summer	various
Vinca, or periwinkle (*Vinca rosea*)	shade, some sun	12 inches	summer	pink, white, mixed
Wishbone flower (*Torenia*)	sun, some shade	12 inches	summer to frost	mixed
Zinnia (*Zinnia elegans*)	sun	24–36 inches	summer to frost	various

PERENNIAL

Flower	Zone	Position	Height	Season	Colors
Adonis (*Adonis vernalis*)	3	sun	10–12 inches	spring	yellow
Alumroot (*see* Coralbells)					
Alyssum (*see* Basket-of-gold)					
Anchusa (*see* Bugloss)					
Anemone, Japanese (*Anemone japonica*)	5	sun, some shade	24–36 inches	late summer to frost	various
Anthemis (*see* Golden marguerite)					
Aster, hardy; or Michaelmas daisy (*Aster novi-belgii*)	4	sun, some shade	6–60 inches	late summer to frost	various
Astilbe, or spiraea (*Astilbe arendsii*)	5	shade	15–30 inches	summer	pink, red, white
Baby's breath (*Gypsophila paniculata*)	3	sun	30–48 inches	summer	pink, white
Balloon flower (*Platycodon grandiflorus*)	3	sun, some shade	12–30 inches	summer	blue, pink, purple, white
Basket-of-gold, or alyssum (*Alyssum saxatile*)	3	sun	8–12 inches	spring	yellow
Bee balm, or bergamot (*Monarda didyma*)	4	sun, some shade	24–36 inches	summer	pink, purple, red, white
Bellflower, or campanula (*Campanula*)	3	sun, some shade	6–36 inches	summer	blue, pink, white
Bergamot (*see* Bee balm)					
Blanket flower, or gaillardia (*Gaillardia aristata*)	3	sun	12–36 inches	summer to frost	brown, orange, red, yellow
Bleeding heart (*Dicentra spectabilis*)	4	shade	24 inches	early spring	pink, red, white

NOTE: "Zone" indicates the coldest region in which a plant can survive (see the Temperature Zone Map on page 168).

Flower	Zone	Position	Height	Season	Colors
Bluebells, virginia (*Mertensia virginica*)	3	shade, some sun	18–24 inches	spring	blue
Blue marguerite (*Felicia amelloides*)	7	sun	12–36 inches	summer to frost	blue
Bugloss, or anchusa (*Anchusa azurea*)	3	shade, some sun	12–48 inches	summer	blue
Butterfly weed (*Asclepias tuberosa*)	4	sun	24–36 inches	summer	orange
Campanula (*see* Bellflower)					
Candytuft, edging (*Iberis sempervirens*)	5	sun, some shade	4–10 inches	spring	pinkish white, white
Cardinal flower (*see* Lobelia)					
Carolina lupine (*see* Thermopsis)					
Catmint (*Nepeta mussinii*)	4	sun	12–24 inches	summer	purple
Christmas rose, or helleborus (*Helleborus niger*)	4	shade, some sun	12–18 inches	late fall to spring	white, turning pinkish green, purple
Chrysanthemum	4	sun	12–60 inches	fall	various
Columbine (*Aquilegia*)	4	sun, some shade	18–36 inches	spring to summer	various
Coneflower, or rudbeckia (*Rudbeckia*)	3	sun	24–60 inches	summer	orange, yellow, mixed
Coralbells, or alumroot (*Heuchera sanguinea*)	3	sun, some shade	12–24 inches	summer	various
Cranesbill geranium (*see* Geranium)					
Daylily (*Hemerocallis*)	5	sun, some shade	18–60 inches	spring, summer, fall	various

Flower	Zone	Position	Height	Season	Colors
Delphinium	3	sun, some shade	18–60 inches	spring, fall	blue, pink, purple, white
Dianthus (*see* Pink)					
Evening primrose (*Oenothera*)	4	sun	12–18 inches	summer	yellow
Feverfew (*Chrysanthemum parthenium*)	3	sun	24–30 inches	summer	creamy yellow
Gaillardia (*see* Blanket flower)					
Gas plant (*Dictamnus albus*)	3	sun	24–30 inches	summer	pink, white
Gayfeather (*Liatris*)	3	sun	18–60 inches	summer to fall	pink, purple, white
Geranium, or cranesbill geranium (*Geranium*)	4	sun, some shade	4–12 inches	summer	various
Globeflower (*Trollius europaeus*)	3	sun, some shade	24–30 inches	spring, early summer	yellow
Globe thistle (*Echinops exaltatus*)	4	sun, some shade	30–48 inches	summer	blue
Gloriosa daisy (*Rudbeckia*)	3	sun	24–36 inches	summer	brown, yellow, mixed
Golden marguerite, or anthemis (*Anthemis tinctoria*)	3	sun, some shade	24–36 inches	summer to frost	yellow
Helleborus (*see* Christmas rose, Lenten rose)					
Hibiscus, or rose mallow (*Hibiscus moscheutos*)	5	sun	36–40 inches	summer to frost	pink, red, white
Iris	3	sun	3–40 inches	spring, summer	various
Kniphofia (*see* Red-hot poker)					

Flower	Zone	Position	Height	Season	Colors
Lenten rose, or helleborus (*Helleborus orientalis*)	4	shade, some sun	12–18 inches	early spring	pink, purple, red, white
Leopard's bane (*Doronicum*)	4	shade, some sun	12–18 inches	spring, fall	yellow
Liatris (*see* Gayfeather)					
Lily-of-the-valley (*Convallaria majalis*)	3	shade	6–8 inches	spring	white
Lobelia, or cardinal flower (*Lobelia cardinalis*)	2	shade	24–30 inches	summer to fall	red
Loosestrife (*Lythrum*)	3	sun, some shade	36–48 inches	summer	pink, purple, red
Lupine (*Lupinus*)	4	sun	36–60 inches	spring, summer	various
Meadowsweet (*Filipendula vulgaris*)	4	sun, some shade	12–24 inches	summer	white
Michaelmas daisy (*see* Aster, hardy)					
Moss pink (*Phlox subulata*)	3	sun	4–6 inches	spring	various
Painted daisy (*Chrysanthemum coccineum*)	4	sun	14–24 inches	summer, sometimes fall	pink, red, white
Peony (*Paeonia*)	3	sun	24–48 inches	spring, summer	various
Phlox, garden (*Phlox paniculata*)	3	sun, some shade	36–48 inches	summer, sometimes fall	pink, purple, red, white
Pink, or dianthus (*Dianthus*)	3	sun	4–18 inches	summer	mixed
Plantain lily (*Hosta*)	3	shade, some sun	4–36 inches	spring, summer, fall	blue, purple, white
Poppy, Iceland (*Papaver nudicaule*)	3	sun	12–24 inches	spring, summer	orange, pink, white, yellow

Flower	Zone	Position	Height	Season	Colors
Poppy, oriental (*Papaver orientale*)	3	sun	36–48 inches	spring, summer	orange, pink, red, white
Primrose (*Primula*)	4	shade	4–12 inches	early spring	various
Red-hot poker, or kniphofia, or tritoma (*Kniphofia*)	4	sun	30–60 inches	summer to frost	orange, red, yellow
Rudbeckia (*see* Coneflower, Gloriosa daisy)					
Sage (*see* Salvia)					
Salvia, or sage (*Salvia*)	4	sun	18–48 inches	summer, fall	blue, purple
Sedum, or stonecrop (*Sedum*)	3	sun, some shade	4–24 inches	spring, summer	various
Shasta daisy (*Chrysanthemum maximum*)	5	sun	12–36 inches	summer	white
Sneezeweed (*Helenium autumnale*)	3	sun	36–48 inches	summer to frost	brown, red, yellow
Speedwell, or veronica (*Veronica*)	3	sun	6–36 inches	summer	pink, blue, white
Spurge (*Euphorbia*)	4	sun	12–14 inches	spring	yellow
Stokes' aster, or stokesia (*Stokesia laevis*)	5	sun	12–15 inches	summer, early fall	blue, purple, white
Stonecrop (*see* Sedum)					
Sunflower (*Helianthus*)	4	sun	36–48 inches	summer to frost	orange, yellow
Thermopsis, or Carolina lupine (*Thermopsis caroliniana*)	3	sun	30–48 inches	summer	yellow

Flower	Zone	Position	Height	Season	Colors
Tickseed (*Coreopsis*)	4	sun	16–36 inches	summer to frost	pink, yellow
Tritoma (*see* Red-hot poker)					
Veronica (*see* Speedwell)					
Viola	6 (some hardier)	sun, some shade	4–6 inches	spring	various
Yarrow (*Achillea*)	3	sun	6–60 inches	summer	red, white, yellow
Yucca	4	sun	36–72 inches	summer	white

Bulbs

Bulbs—a group of horticultural beauties that includes true bulbs, such as daffodils and hyacinths; corms, such as crocuses and gladiolus; and tuberous roots and rhizomes like dahlias and calla lilies—play an important role in any year-round garden. Like perennials, they offer almost guaranteed long-term beauty for little effort and provide welcome spring, summer, fall, and (in milder climates) winter color. Golden winter aconite and creamy galanthus spring bravely up through drifts of snow; autumn-flowering crocuses bring scent and color to the garden as the year wanes. Like the annuals, bulbs are adaptable, for they can be moved about from season to season, giving flexibility to the garden plan. They grow well in all kinds of soil except powdery sand and wet, soggy clay, and for shady areas there are bulbs such as Siberian squills, crocuses, tuberous begonias, and lilies-of-the-Nile.

Some bulbs are hardy.* They are usually planted in the fall, for they need cold weather to grow successfully, and they can be left in the ground in temperate areas for several seasons or, in some cases, for many years. In northern regions, tender bulbs that bloom in summer are planted in spring, then dug up and stored when nights grow short and chilly.

Before choosing bulbs for your garden, browse through the many excellent catalogues put out yearly by bulbsmen. There is an enormous selection available to you within some of the species. Tulips come in a dazzling bouquet of colors and range in height from the dainty six-inch Greigis to the stately thirty-inch Darwins. They bloom from early to late spring. Use the medium-sized ones, perhaps, to make a graceful transition

---

* Some so-called hardy bulbs are not hardy everywhere. Your invaluable local nurseryman and your friends with established gardens can tell you which ones are safe to plant in your area.

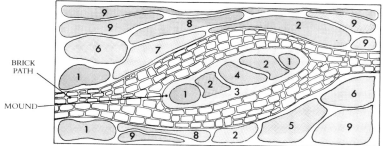

1. Hyacinths (*Hyacinthus orientalis*)

2. Tulips (*Tulipa saxatilis*)

3. Tulips (*Tulipa pulchella*)

4. Petticoat narcissus (*Narcissus bulbocodium*)

5. Tulips (*Tulipa* 'Pink Supreme')

6. Daffodils (*Narcissus* 'Lady Bird')

7. Grape hyacinths (*Muscari armeniacum*)

8. Anemones (*Anemone blanda atrocaerulea*)

9. Tulips (*Tulipa* 'Aristocrat')

from ground cover to a flowering tree, the largest in massed plantings or to thread orchestrated color through a spring border. Daffodils offer a palette of yellows and whites, and, as is true also of tulips, there are several attractive forms to choose from. They are friendly flowers, mixing happily with other species, such as wood hyacinths, grape hyacinths, and pansies. Garden hyacinths vary little in form but much in color: pink, purple, white, blue, and yellow. A display of them is superb in any sunny location, but their splendid fragrance will delight you, too, if you plant them near a place where you are apt to walk.

Don't overlook the more unusual hardy bulbs tucked away at the back of the catalogues. Tall purple alliums bring an exotic touch to the garden, and papery anemones are enchanting along a path and sprinkled among perennials in a border.

Formal plantings of hardy bulbs are beautiful but you can also naturalize them or make them look as though they were growing wild. Take a handful, toss them gently down, and plant them where they fall. Daffodils, crocuses, and grape hyacinths are good candidates for this treatment, and they will keep coming up for years where you planted them. Remember that the smaller the bulb, the more of them you will need to make an effect. Tiny flowers like Siberian squills and winter aconites look their best in drifts of at least three dozen plants.

Bulbs belong in the mixed border, especially in the early spring when little else is in bloom, but plant the long-leaved varieties behind perennials that will shoot up in early summer and hide them from view.

The summer-flowering bulbs come in exotic colors and shapes: the spidery Peruvian daffodil and gloriosa lily, the ballerina-like peacock orchid. Rich pink leaves of elephant's ear give the border a junglelike beauty. But there are also many old-fashioned favorites like dahlias and begonias to deck the summer border.

1. Azaleas (*Rhododendron*, Exbury hybrid)

2. Iris (*Iris* 'Deep Space')

3. Lilies (*Lilium auratum* 'Pink Glory Strain')

4. Iris (*Iris* 'Far Out')

5. Peonies (*Paeonia* 'Pink Lemonade')

6. Daylilies (*Hemerocallis* 'Flaming Dawn')

7. Daylilies (*Hemerocallis* 'Little Papoose')

8. Iris (*Iris* 'Banbury Ruffles')

9. Peonies (*Paeonia* 'Judy Ann')

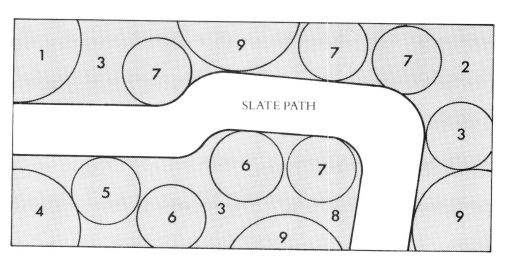

Some of the later flowering bulbs, including the hardy lilies and the tender gladiolus, come in so many varieties you can count on a progression of bloom through the summer months. Selecting the colors you want for the time and place you want them is as pleasantly brain-teasing as a crossword—and in the end you have much more than a pencilled-in puzzle to show for it.

Bulb Care

The first and most important rule is to buy only top-quality bulbs. Avoid any material that does not come from reputable dealers. If you cannot plant immediately, be sure to store your new bulbs in a dry, cool place. All bulbs do best in organic, moisture-retaining but rapidly draining soil.

Summer-flowering bulbs need to be planted only a few inches below ground, but, because they have to survive cold weather, hardy bulbs must be planted deep: from three inches for snowdrops to eight inches for tulips. Plant hardy bulbs to the depth recommended on the package they came in. "Three inches deep" means that the base of the bulb should be at least three inches below ground level. When hardy bulbs are planted in a perennial border, put them in deep enough so you will not hurt them accidentally while cultivating; in well-drained, loose soil, crocus bulbs may be planted as deep as eight inches, tulips as deep as twelve inches. Dig round holes, making sure the bottom is saucer-shaped rather than **V**-shaped to avoid trapping air below the bulb. Spill a handful of bonemeal or bulb fertilizer into the hole and slip the hardy bulb in, growing side up: that is, with the pointed end (or the one showing growth) at the top. Firm the soil over the bulb; do not leave it loose.

Very early flowering hardy bulbs, like winter aconite and dogtooth violet, should be planted at the end of August or early in September; other spring bulbs should go into the ground at such time in September or later as to give them three months in the ground until growth begins. In frost-free areas, hardy bulbs must be dug up each year and refrigerated (at 40°–50° F) to simulate the winter conditions they need to survive.

Hardy bulbs can live off their own storehouses of food for some time, but they must be attended to when they are in active growth. Water them regularly from the time they start growing until after the flowers fade. Then taper watering off gradually. Dormant bulbs need only the water natural conditions provide. You will give established spring-flowering bulbs a boost if you fertilize them once a season. Never cut or mow off foliage after they have bloomed, for the leaves provide food for the bulb. Let them ripen, then cut when the plant has yellowed.

Plant summer-flowering bulbs outside after all danger of frost is over. Give them a complete fertilizer as soon as growth appears and again in the few weeks before they bloom. Use a balanced feeding mix that has little nitrogen. Some summer bulbs, like tuberous begonias, lilies-of-the-Nile, and calla lilies, can be given a head start in flats indoors before they are put out in the garden.

In most of the United States, summer-flowering bulbs must be dug up in fall and stored through the winter; however, you can leave them in the ground if temperatures in your area do not drop below freezing. After the foliage stops growing in the fall, dig up summer bulbs, hose off any dirt, and let them dry in an airy place. Cut off to about three inches any foliage that has not fallen. Store them in a dry, cool place (about 50° F) in boxes of dry sand or peat moss, on open trays, or in brown paper bags.

Bulbs

FALL-PLANTED

Bulb	Position	Height	Season	Depth to Plant
Allium (*Allium giganteum*)	sun	48–60 inches	summer	8 inches
Anemone, or windflower (*Anemone blanda*)	shade, some sun	2–8 inches	early spring	4 inches
Brodiaea	sun	6–18 inches	spring	3 inches
Camassia	shade, some sun	18–36 inches	spring	4 inches
Chionodoxa (*see* Glory-of-the-snow)				
Colchium (*Colchium autumnale*)	sun, some shade	5–10 inches	fall	5 inches
Crocus	sun, some shade	3–5 inches	spring, fall	4 inches
Crown imperial, or fritillaria (*Fritillaria imperalis*)	sun, some shade	24–30 inches	spring	6 inches
Daffodil (*Narcissus*)	sun, some shade	6–20 inches	early–mid-spring	8 inches
Dogtooth violet (*Erythronium*)	shade	10–14 inches	late winter, early spring	4 inches
Eranthis (*see* Winter aconite)				
Fall daffodil, or sternbergia (*Sternbergia lutea*)	sun	4 inches	fall	5 inches
Foxtail lily (*Eremurus*)	sun	3–12 feet	spring	6 inches
Fritillaria (*see* Crown imperial)				
Galanthus (*see* Snowdrop)				

158

Bulb	Position	Height	Season	Depth to Plant
Glory-of-the-snow, or chionodoxa (*Chionodoxa luciliae*)	sun	6 inches	spring	4 inches
Grape hyacinth (*Muscari*)	sun, shade	6–10 inches	spring	3 inches
Hardy amaryllis (*Lycoris squamigera*)	sun, some shade	24–36 inches	summer	5 inches
Hyacinth (*Hyacinthus orientalis*)	sun, some shade	6–15 inches	spring	8 inches
Iris, Dutch (*Iris xiphium*)	sun, some shade	16–18 inches	late spring	8 inches
Iris, dwarf (*Iris reticulata*)	sun	4–6 inches	early spring	4 inches
Jonquil (*see* Narcissus)				
Lily, hardy (*Lilium*)	varies	12–72 inches	summer	varies
Mariposa lily (*Calochortus*)	sun	18–24 inches	spring	3 inches
Narcissus, or jonquil (*Narcissus*)	sun	4–18 inches	early–mid-spring	6 inches
Siberian squill (*Scilla siberica*)	sun, some shade	5–6 inches	early spring	4 inches
Snowdrop, or galanthus (*Galanthus*)	sun, some shade	4–6 inches	late winter, early spring	3 inches
Snowflake (*Leucojum*)	shade	6–12 inches	early spring, late spring, fall	4 inches
Spanish bluebell (*see* Wood hyacinth)				
Star-of-Bethlehem (*Ornithogalum umbellatum*)	sun, some shade	6–8 inches	spring	2 inches

Bulb	Position	Height	Season	Depth to Plant
Sternbergia (*see* Fall daffodil)				
Toad lily (*Fritillaria meleagris*)	sun, some shade	10–12 inches	early spring	4 inches
Tulip (*Tulipa*)	sun	6–30 inches	spring	8 inches
Windflower (*see* Anemone)				
Winter aconite, or eranthis (*Eranthis hyemalis*)	shade, some sun	3–5 inches	late winter, early spring	4 inches
Wood hyacinth, or Spanish bluebell (*Endymion hispanicus*)	sun, some shade	12–20 inches	spring	5 inches

SPRING-PLANTED

Bulb	Position	Height	Season	Depth to Plant
Begonia, tuberous (*Begonia tuberosa*)	shade, some sun	8–12 inches	summer	1/2-inch
Calla lily (*Zantedeschia*)	sun, some shade	18–30 inches	summer	3 inches
Canna lily (*Canna*)	sun	40–72 inches	summer	4 inches
Dahlia	sun	15–72 inches	late spring, summer to frost	3 inches
Elephant's ear (*Caladium*)	shade, some sun	12–24 inches	summer	1–2 inches
Gladiolus	sun	20–50 inches	summer	6 inches
Gloriosa lily (*Gloriosa*)	sun	4–10 feet (climbs)	summer	4 inches
Lily-of-the-Nile (*Agapanthus africanus*)	sun, some shade	18–22 inches	summer	2 inches
Montbretia (*Tritoma*)	sun	24 inches	summer to frost	4 inches
Peacock orchid (*Acidanthera bicolor*)	sun	24–36 inches	summer	3 inches
Peruvian daffodil (*Hymenocallis narcissiflora*)	sun, some shade	24 inches	summer	3 inches
Ranunculus, tuberous (*Ranunculus asiaticus*)	sun	16–18 inches	summer to frost	2 inches
Summer hyacinth (*Galtonia candicans*)	sun	24–36 inches	summer	5–6 inches
Tiger flower (*Tigridia pavonia*)	sun	24–32 inches	summer to frost	4 inches
Tuberose (*Polyanthes tuberosa*)	sun	24–32 inches	summer	3 inches

Vines

Vines can break up the monotony of bare walls, soften sterile lines, deck walls or fences, or block out objectionable views. They fit into small spaces and assume many shapes. Flowering vines can make breathtaking effects. Vines are perfect for pergolas, and they add color to the garden. Many gardeners complain that vines require continual pruning and attention, but this is a drawback only with vines that are rampant growers, which will indeed take over an area unless trained.

There are many vines that stay within bounds with little care. Some of the high-climbers—clematis and bougainvillea—are delightful screens of living color. Stephanotis, wisteria, and sweet pea have a fragile loveliness. And many vines, including bittersweet and trumpet honeysuckle, have colorful winter berries that give welcome color to a snowy landscape.

Because of their high soot toleration and general hardiness, some vines make excellent city dwellers. Among the annuals, the very hardy garden nasturtium is a fine choice for screening and covering trellises and fences. The perennial bower actinidia, English ivy, silver-lace vine, and American bittersweet are shade tolerant, and the trumpet vine triumphs in the worst kinds of air pollution.

Annual vines, like annual flowers, grow quickly and make wonderful screens and fillers. They die in winter in areas that are not frost-free. Start them early indoors or, if they are fast growers, sow seed after the ground has warmed up. Some perennial vines are evergreen, some deciduous, and you should bear this in mind when selecting them. You can grow the perennials from seed or root cuttings, too, but for quick results, purchase established plants in pots.

Place rooted woody vines in a hole dug to a depth of three to four feet, so the roots will have ample space to grow. Half-fill the hole with water and put the plant in place. Replace the dug-out soil with good topsoil, but do not add manure or fertilizers, which might burn the plants. Gently tamp down the earth around the collar of the plant so that air pockets will not form. Water again, thoroughly and deeply. For the first few weeks, keep an eye on the plant to see that it is getting started. Once it is established, routine care is sufficient. Prune, thin, and shape all vines regularly to keep them looking handsome.

Certain vines climb by twining their stems around slender supports such as string or latticework. Others have clinging tendrils, others adhesive disks or rootlike appendages that help the plant support itself. These disks and appendages can damage wooden walls. Many vines, even the twining woody ones, need support, so, before choosing a vine, find out whether or not it will need any.

Some varieties of perennial and annual flowers and some shrubs are prostrate in growth (ivy geranium and trailing lantana, for example), and they make wonderful ground cover. Vines may be open and delicate or heavy with masses of foliage. Select carefully to achieve the effect you want.

A Treasury of Vines

ANNUAL

Vine	Position	Habit	Conspicuous Flowers	Use
Balloon vine (*Cardiospermum halicacabum*)	sun	climbs to 12 feet	white—summer	fence, screen, trellis
Black-eyed susan (*Thunbergia alata*)	sun, shade	climbs, trails to 15 feet	orange, white, yellow—summer	ground cover, trellis
Canary-bird flower, or canary creeper (*Tropaeolum perigrinum*)	shade, some sun	climbs to 10 feet	yellow—summer	trellis
Cardinal climber (*Ipomoea multifida*)	sun	climbs to 20 feet	red—summer to frost	trellis
Cathedral bells, or cup-and-saucer vine (*Cobaea scandens*)	sun	climbs to 20 feet	purple, white—spring, summer	shade, trellis
Cypress vine (*Quamoclit pennata*)	sun	climbs to 20 feet	red—summer	trellis
Dutchman's pipe (*Aristolochia durior*)	shade, sun	climbs to 30 feet		screen, shade, trellis
Hyacinth bean (*Dolichos lablab*)	sun	climbs 15 to 30 feet	purple, white—summer	fence, trellis
Japanese hop vine (*Humulus japonicus*)	sun	climbs to 10 feet		fence, screen, shade
Morning glory (*Ipomoea purpurea*)	sun	climbs 15 to 20 feet	many colors—summer	fence, screen, trellis
Nasturtium, garden (*Tropaeolum majus*)	sun	climbs, trails to 10 feet	orange, red, yellow—summer to frost	ground cover, fence, trellis; city garden
Scarlet runner bean (*Phaseolus coccineus*)	sun	climbs to 10 feet	red—summer	wall (with support), trellis
Sweet pea (*Lathyrus odoratus*)	sun	climbs to 6 feet	many colors—summer	screen (with support)

NOTE: This list includes plants commonly treated as annuals.

PERENNIAL

Vine	Zone	Position	Habit	Conspicuous Flowers	Use
Actinidia, bower; or Tara vine (*Actinidia arguta*)	5	sun, some shade	climbs to 20 feet		screen; city garden
Akebia (*see* Chocolate vine)					
Allamanda (*Allamanda cathartica*)	9	sun	climbs to 40 feet; evergreen	yellow—summer	fence, wall (with support)
Bittersweet, American (*Celastrus scandens*)	4	sun, some shade	climbs, trails to 20 feet; red berries		ground cover, wall (with support); city garden
Bittersweet, oriental (*Celastrus orbiculatus*)	5	sun, some shade	climbs, trails to 30 feet; red, yellow berries		ground cover, wall (with support)
Boston ivy, or Japanese creeper (*Parthenocissus tricuspidata*)	5	sun, shade	climbs to 50 feet; blue berries		brick or stone wall
Bougainvillea	9	sun	climbs to 50 feet	purple, red, orange, white—spring, summer	screen, trellis
Cape honeysuckle (*Tecomaria capensis*)	9	sun	climbs to 6 feet; evergreen	orange, red, yellow—summer, fall	trellis
Carolina jessamine (*Gelsemium sempervirens*)	7	sun	climbs to 20 feet; evergreen	yellow—spring, summer	trellis, brick or stone wall
Chocolate vine, or akebia (*Akebia quinata*)	5	sun, shade	climbs to 20 feet; semievergreen	purple—spring	trellis, wall (with support)
Clematis, jackmani	6	shade, sun	climbs to 10 feet	purple—summer	fence, screen, trellis
Clematis, sweet autumn (*Clematis paniculata*)	5	shade, sun	climbs to 30 feet	white—late summer	screen, wall

NOTE: "Zone" indicates the coldest region in which a plant can survive (see the Temperature Zone Map on page 168).

Perennial Vines

Vine	Zone	Position	Habit	Conspicuous Flowers	Use
Clock vine, or sky flower (*Thunbergia grandiflora*)	8	sun	climbs to 10 feet; evergreen	blue—summer, fall	trellis
Coral vine (*Antigonon leptopus*)	9	sun	climbs to 30 feet	pink, white—spring to late fall	fence, wall (with support)
Evergreen bittersweet (*see* Winter creeper)					
Fig, creeping (*Ficus pumila*)	9	sun	climbs to 30 feet; evergreen; yellowish fruit (inedible)		wall (with support)
Honeysuckle, Hall's Japanese (*Lonicera japonica halliana*)	5	sun, shade	climbs to 30 feet; semievergreen; black berries	white, yellow—spring	ground cover, trellis
Honeysuckle, trumpet (*Lonicera sempervirens*)	4	sun, shade	climbs to 50 feet; semievergreen; red berries	orange-red—summer	ground cover, screen
Hydrangea, climbing (*Hydrangea anomala petiolaris*)	5	sun, some shade	climbs to 40 feet	white—summer	brick or stone wall, ground cover
Ivy, Boston (*see* Boston ivy)					
Ivy, English (*Hedera helix*)	6	shade, some sun	climbs to 80 feet; evergreen		brick or stone wall, ground cover; city garden
Japanese creeper (*see* Boston ivy)					
Jasmine, Arabian (*Jasminum sambac*)	9	sun	climbs to 12 feet	white, purple—summer	trellis, wall (with support)
Kadsura, Japanese (*Kadsura japonica*)	7	sun	climbs to 15 feet; semievergreen; red berries	white—summer	trellis, wall (with support)
Madagascar jasmine (*see* Stephanotis)					

Vine	Zone	Position	Habit	Conspicuous Flowers	Use
Passion flower (*Passiflora caerulea*)	8	sun	climbs to 20 feet; semievergreen; orange fruit (inedible)	blue, white— summer	ground cover, wall (with support)
Rose, climbing (*Rosa*)	4	sun	climbs to 8 feet	pink, red, white—spring	bank, fence, trellis (with support)
Silver-lace vine (*Polygonum auberti*)	4	sun, shade	climbs 15 to 20 feet	white—summer, fall	fence, trellis; city garden
Sky flower (*see* Clock vine)					
Star jasmine (*Trachelospermum jasminoides*)	9	shade	climbs to 10 feet	white—spring, summer	trellis, wall (with support)
Stephanotis, or Madagascar jasmine (*Stephanotis floribunda*)	9	sun, some shade	climbs to 6 feet	white—spring, summer	trellis
Tara vine (*see* Actinidia, bower)					
Trumpet vine (*Campsis radicans*)	5	sun, shade	climbs to 30 feet	orange, red, yellow—summer	ground cover, stone or brick wall; city garden
Wax plant (*Hoya carnosa*)	9	sun	climbs to 10 feet	pink, white— spring, summer	trellis
Winter creeper, or evergreen bittersweet (*Euonymus fortunei*)	6	sun	climbs, trails to 6 feet; evergreen; red, yellow berries		brick or stone wall
Wisteria, Chinese (*Wisteria sinensis*)	5	sun	climbs to 100 feet	blue, purple— spring	wall
Wisteria, Japanese (*Wisteria floribunda*)	5	sun	climbs to 25 feet	pink, purple, red, white-- spring	wall

Temperature Zone Map

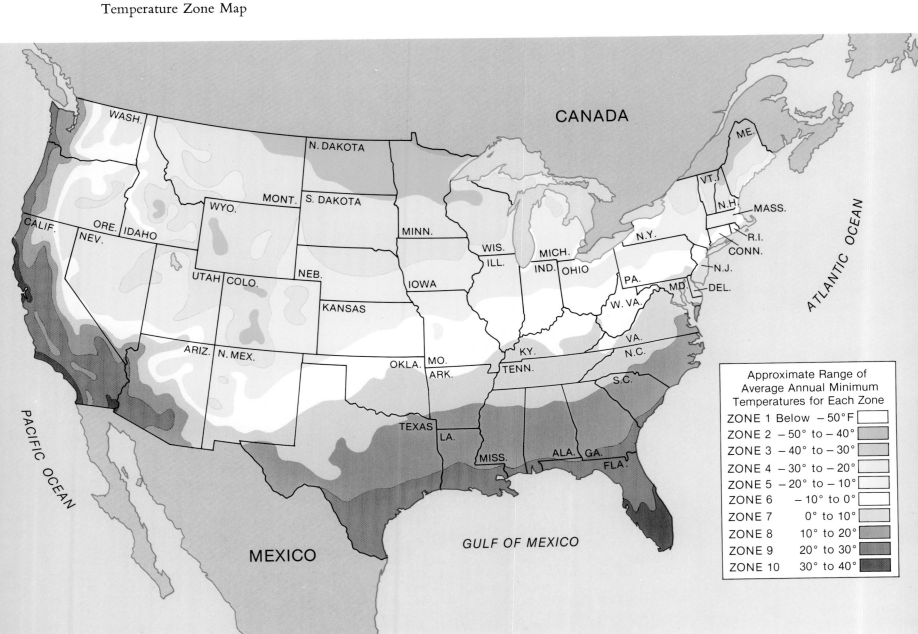

Approximate Range of
Average Annual Minimum
Temperatures for Each Zone

ZONE 1	Below −50°F	
ZONE 2	−50° to −40°	
ZONE 3	−40° to −30°	
ZONE 4	−30° to −20°	
ZONE 5	−20° to −10°	
ZONE 6	−10° to 0°	
ZONE 7	0° to 10°	
ZONE 8	10° to 20°	
ZONE 9	20° to 30°	
ZONE 10	30° to 40°	

6. REGIONAL GARDENING

Whether you live in the East, the Middle West, the South, or the West, your garden can be enjoyed in all seasons of the year. However, each region has its own climate, and knowing something about your weather is a basic part of good gardening. The most widely used reference guide to growing plants in the United States is the temperature zone map prepared by the Agricultural Research Service of the United States Department of Agriculture. Based on average minimum night temperatures as reported by weather stations, it divides North America into ten zones and is very helpful in predicting the adaptability of plants to specific climates.

Of course, temperature zone maps do not reflect climate differences within zones: differences between hills and valleys or between inland locations and places near bodies of water. Thermal belts and fog belts cause temperatures to vary, too. There are some places in northern California where specific conditions exist in only a five-to-ten-mile radius; outside such regions, temperatures may be five to ten degrees lower, winds stronger, and other conditions different, as well. You should consult your neighbors and, as always, a local nursery about the exact conditions that prevail where you live.

A plant that survives without injury the climatic extremes of a given area is called hardy. Plants that are hardy in one area may not be hardy in another. Frost is not the only temperature extreme to consider. Many plants need a long, cold rest in winter; too much heat then will kill or discourage them. Peonies, for example, do not do well in the South, and hardy bulbs like the narcissus must be refrigerated before planting in the Deep South.

But, when plant hardiness is mentioned, usually it is resistance to cold that is meant.

Some plants can withstand freezing temperatures. Tender plants cannot do this. When temperature drops quickly and a plant's tissues freeze quickly, ice crystals form and the plant may die or die down to the ground ("winter kill"). When temperatures fall gradually, the plant's tissues freeze slowly and can recuperate, provided it does not happen too many times. Repeated freezings and thawings increase the danger of injury.

To survive freezing, hardy plants must make steady growth through the growing season, with a gradual cessation from mid-August until the first killing frost. Late growth can cause plants to be unfit to survive winter. Starting in late summer, cultivation and watering must be decreased. Do not feed plants in late summer either. Late feeding with high-nitrogen fertilizers can force succulent growth and reduce hardiness of many plants, including roses and broad-leaved evergreens. Plants that lose their leaves because of insects or disease are especially vulnerable to premature freezing.

Summer mulches should be removed in fall and replaced before winter weather starts (permanent mulching can reduce hardiness of plants by keeping the soil temperature warm late in the season). Winter mulches give protection from rapid sequences of freezing and thawing, and they keep soil moist, increasing the hardiness of plants. Evergreens and deciduous trees and shrubs lose water through their stems all winter. The stronger the wind, the greater the loss, and when the ground is frozen, the plant is unable to absorb water and to replenish the lost moisture.

To help you choose perennial flowers, shrubs, and trees that are hardy in your area, most garden catalogues indicate the northernmost zone in which each plant they carry can survive. Annuals, which flower and die in one season, may be planted in any area without regard for regional variations of temperature, though certain ones—like lupines—prefer cool nights and thus do better north of zone 6, while others—like petunias and ageratum—

will not come to maturity before frost in northern zones if their seed is sown directly in the garden ofter the last frost in spring.

Hardiness influences your choice of plants, but it need not stop you from experimenting. Your garden can include several plants that are not supposed to be able to grow in your region, if they are strategically placed. Bougainvilleas need warmth in winter and, in zone 8, may survive if protected by southern house walls. In the South, lilacs may flourish in more exposed places, where they can get the coolness they require.

If you buy plants from a supplier in a warmer (or much cooler) climate than your own, be sure the species is hardy in your zone. Remember, you can modify your zone somewhat by adjusting the locations of plants within your garden. But if you would rather not be bothered protecting borderline-hardy plants against winter stress, choose plants listed in catalogues as being hardy in a zone somewhat colder than your own.

Seasonal Care

The North

MARCH, APRIL, MAY

Do general garden cleanup; remove winter mulch gradually

Prune trees, roses, and fruit trees; shape hedges in March and April

Plant trees and shrubs before new growth begins

Start new lawns and reseed old ones

Begin overall plant-feeding program after the ground thaws; start
feeding perennials when they are four inches high

Sow annual, biennial, and perennial seed when the ground has
warmed up

Divide existing perennials and replant them

Do dormant spraying of fruit trees

Plant tender annual seedlings, summer-flowering bulbs, and
wintered-over plants outside after last frost

Mulch broad-leaved evergreens to improve water retention; apply
acid fertilizer to azaleas and rhododendrons

JUNE, JULY, AUGUST

Sow annual seed in June for late summer bloom

Prune, cultivate, mulch, and water roses

Cut back perennials that have bloomed

Pinch back chrysanthemums to make them bushy

Be sure all plants (lawns, shrubs, perennials, biennials, annuals)
are thoroughly watered through the summer

Weed and cultivate annuals, perennials, and biennials; remove
flowers as they fade

Continue to fertilize plants until mid-August
Plant summer-flowering bulbs until mid-June
Prune spring-flowering shrubs after they bloom
Trim evergreen hedges
Cut and hang herbs to dry
Plant certain lily varieties in August

SEPTEMBER, OCTOBER, NOVEMBER
Start new lawns and reseed old ones
Plant certain kinds of spring bulbs in October
Plant perennial and biennial seeds and seedlings
Mulch roses in November and plant and mulch new roses
Dig up and store tender bulbs
Plant trees and shrubs
Do general cleanup before snow starts: turn over
    beds, mow lawns
Cover beds with mulching material in November
Water evergreens before the ground freezes

DECEMBER, JANUARY, FEBRUARY
Provide protection from freezing and thawing by covering
    perennials and low evergreens with branches of spruce, pine, or
    cedar
Remove snow from evergreens but do not remove ice if it forms:
    let it melt
Replant perennials as best you can if they heave out of the soil
Do some light pruning of deciduous plants in February if the weather
    permits
Sow annual seed indoors in February
Look over garden catalogues; make plans for the new season

The Pacific Coast

MARCH, APRIL, MAY
    Do general garden cleanup
    Plant magnolias, rhododendrons, and other broad-leaved evergreens
       in March
    Prune peaches and almonds in March
    Prune spring-flowering shrubs after they bloom
    Shape hedges
    Divide summer-blooming perennials
    Sow summer annual seed in April or May, depending on your climate,
       and set out bedding plants in May
    Start watering in northern California in April
    Sow seed of perennials and biennials from May through July
    Plant summer-flowering bulbs
    Prune fuchsias
    Begin overall plant-feeding program
    Mulch trees and shrubs and apply acid fertilizers to camellias,
       azaleas, and rhododendrons; be sure all broad-leaved evergreens
       get plenty of water
    Start new lawns and reseed old ones

JUNE, JULY, AUGUST
    Mulch plants to retain moisture
    Finish setting out bedding plants in June
    Weed and cultivate annuals, perennials, and biennials; remove
       flowers as they fade
    Change plantings of winter annuals for warm-weather flowers in
       northern California
    Plant asters, petunias, and zinnias in southern California

Keep watering, because it is dry in the Pacific Northwest in July;
   water and water is the rule in northern California
Continue to fertilize plants
Make final plantings of dahlias and gladiolus
Sow perennial and biennial seed for winter and spring bloom in
   northern California
Plant summer-flowering bulbs in August
Prune deciduous and evergreen trees in August in the Pacific
   Northwest
Cut back and fertilize those perennials at the end of their bloom
   that will bloom again in the fall
Cut and hang herbs to dry

SEPTEMBER, OCTOBER, NOVEMBER
Begin fall cleanup: turn over beds, mow lawns
Fertilize roses
Start new lawns and reseed old ones
Water often in dry areas
Dig and store tender bulbs, plant fall- and spring-blooming bulbs,
   plant roses, mulch fuchsias, plant trees and shrubs in the Pacific
   Northwest
Install bedding plants, plant trees, shrubs, and spring-flowering bulbs,
   dig and store tender bulbs in northern California
Plant seeds of sweet peas and calendulas for winter bloom, set
   spring-flowering bulbs in the ground, set out annual plants in
   southern California
Plant annuals for winter bloom in northern California, for early
   spring flowering in the Pacific Northwest
Look over garden catalogues; make plans for the new season

DECEMBER, JANUARY, FEBRUARY

Prune trees and shrubs, plant trees and roses in March in the Pacific
Northwest

Plant roses, deciduous shrubs and trees, and perennials in January,
when you may also prune, in California

Sow annual seed in January and February

Fertilize lawns by February

Do dormant spraying of shrubs and fruit trees

Prune spring-flowering shrubs after they bloom

The South

MARCH, APRIL, MAY

    Feed spring-flowering bulbs as they start to grow
    Plant trees and shrubs
    Sow annual seed outdoors; set annual plants in beds in mid-April
        or earlier
    Prune spring-flowering shrubs after they bloom
    Mulch broad-leaved evergreens to improve water retention; apply
        acid fertilizer to azaleas and rhododendrons
    Dig, divide, and plant perennials
    Prune roses; do light pruning of boxwood and other evergreens
    Start new lawns and reseed old ones; mow regularly
    Fertilize lawns, shrubs, and roses
    Plant summer-flowering bulbs after all danger of frost is over
    Plant azaleas
    Be sure to water plants: May can be dry
    Pinch back chrysanthemums to make them bushy, from May
        through July
    Sow perennial and biennial seed from May through July

JUNE, JULY, AUGUST

    Cut back and fertilize those perennials at the end of their bloom
        that will bloom again in the fall
    Water all plants thoroughly; apply a summer mulch
    Trim hedges after new growth develops
    Prune azaleas lightly in June
    Fertilize lawns in July; mow regularly
    Weed and cultivate annuals, perennials, and biennials; remove
        flowers as they fade
    Divide and transplant perennials

Sow annual seed for fall flowers

Sow seed of some perennial and biennial species in August for
 next year's garden

Cut and hang herbs to dry

SEPTEMBER, OCTOBER, NOVEMBER

Set out pansies and winter annuals in September

Divide crowded perennials if you have not done so earlier

Plant spring-flowering bulbs from September to December,
 depending on your climate

Sow seed of hardy annuals

Start new lawns and reseed old ones (start winter lawns of frost-
 resistant annual grasses during the first cool spell)

Plant trees and shrubs in October and November; plant roses in
 November and December and fertilize them then

Protect plants with mulch, as November is frost time in some parts
 of the South; dig up and store tender bulbs in these areas

Do general cleanup: turn over beds, mow lawns

Look over garden catalogues; make plans for the new season

DECEMBER, JANUARY, FEBRUARY

Plant trees and shrubs in January and February in the Deep South

Do some winter pruning but do not prune spring-flowering shrubs
 until they have bloomed

Shape hedges

Plant daffodil bulbs if you have not yet done so

Plant deciduous trees, shrubs, roses, and vines in the Deep South

Prune established roses and spray them

Sow seed of annuals that like cool weather: alyssum, California
 poppies, larkspurs, lupines

Plant magnolias in February

Do dormant spraying of fruit trees
Do general garden cleanup in February
Plant certain kinds of summer-blooming bulbs in the
   Deep South: calla lilies, tuberous begonias
Fertilize camellias and azaleas after they flower
Fertilize lawns

7. CHOOSING AND CARING FOR PLANTS

Flower beds, beautifully balanced by sculptured hedges, are set off by flowering trees in the Whitney Stone garden in Charlottesville.

181

CHOOSE FLOWERS BY COLOR

ANNUALS AND BIENNIALS

Blue

Baby snapdragon (*Linaria faucicola*)
Bachelor's button, or cornflower (*Centaurea cyanus*)
Blue cupflower (*Nierembergia caerulea*)
Blue lace flower (*Trachymene caerulea*)
Browallia
Butterfly flower (*Schizanthus*)
Canterbury bells (*Campanula medium*)
China aster (*Callistephus chinensis*)
Dwarf morning glory (*Convolvulus tricolor*)
Flossflower, or ageratum (*Ageratum houstonianum*)
Forget-me-not (*Myosotis sylvatica*)
Heliotrope (*Heliotropium*)
Larkspur (*Consolida ambigua*)
Lobelia, edging (*Lobelia erinus*)
Love-in-a-mist, or nigella (*Nigella damascena*)
Lupine (*Lupinus hartwegii*)
Morning glory (*Ipomoea purpurea*)
Nemesia
Pansy (*Viola wittrockiana*)
Petunia
Phlox (*Phlox drummondii*)
Pincushion flower (*Scabiosa atropurpurea*)
Salvia, or sage (*Salvia*)
Sea lavender, or statice (*Limonium*)
Stock (*Matthiola*)

Vervain (*Verbena*)
Viper's bugloss (*Echium*)
Wishbone flower (*Torenia*)

Bronze

African daisy (*Arctotis*)
Chrysanthemum
Marigold (*Tagetes*)
Sunflower (*Helianthus*)
Tickseed, or calliopsis (*Coreopsis*)
Zinnia (*Zinnia elegans*)

Orange

African daisy (*Arctotis*)
California poppy (*Eschscholzia californica*)
Cape marigold (*Dimorphotheca pluvialis*)
Chrysanthemum
Cockscomb (*Celosia argentea*)
Dahlia
Impatiens, or balsam (*Impatiens balsamina*)
Lantana
Marigold (*Tagetes*)
Nasturtium (*Tropaeolum*)
Nemesia
Painted tongue (*Salpiglossis sinuata*)
Pansy (*Viola wittrockiana*)
Poppy, Shirley (*Papaver rhoeas*)
Portulaca, or rose moss, or sun moss (*Portulaca*

grandiflora)
Pot marigold (*Calendula officinalis*)
Snapdragon (*Antirrhinum*)
Sunflower (*Helianthus*)
Tickseed, or calliopsis (*Coreopsis*)
Transvaal daisy (*Gerbera jamesonii*)
Zinnia (*Zinnia elegans*)

Pink, Rose

Acroclinium (*Helipterum manglesii*)
Baby's breath (*Gypsophila elegans*)
Baby snapdragon (*Linaria faucicola*)
Bachelor's button, or cornflower (*Centaurea cyanus*)
Begonia, wax (*Begonia semperflorens cultorum*)
Butterfly flower (*Schizanthus*)
California poppy (*Eschscholzia californica*)
Candytuft, common (*Iberis umbellata*)
Candytuft, rocket (*Iberis amara*)
Canterbury bells (*Campanula medium*)
Carnation (*Dianthus caryophyllus*)
China aster (*Callistephus chinensis*)
Clarkia
Cockscomb (*Celosia argentea*)
Cosmos
Dahlia
Dwarf morning glory (*Convolvulus tricolor*)
English daisy (*Bellis perennis*)
Farewell-to-spring, or godetia (*Godetia amoena*)

Flossflower, or ageratum (*Ageratum houstonianum*)
Forget-me-not (*Myosotis sylvatica*)
Four o'clock (*Mirabilis jalapa*)
Foxglove (*Digitalis purpurea*)
Geranium, or pelargonium (*Pelargonium*)
Globe amaranth (*Gomphrena globosa*)
Hollyhock (*Althaea rosea*)
Ice plant (*Mesembryanthemum crystallinum*)
Impatiens, or balsam (*Impatiens balsamina*)
Larkspur (*Consolida ambigua*)
Lobelia, edging (*Lobelia erinus*)
Love-in-a-mist, or nigella (*Nigella damascena*)
Lupine (*Lupinus hartwegii*)
Morning glory (*Ipomoea purpurea*)
Nemesia
Painted tongue (*Salpiglossis sinuata*)
Pansy (*Viola wittrockiana*)
Petunia
Phlox (*Phlox drummondii*)
Pincushion flower (*Scabiosa atropurpurea*)
Pink (*Dianthus*)
Poppy, Shirley (*Papaver rhoeas*)
Portulaca, or rose moss, or sun moss (*Portulaca grandiflora*)
Primrose, fairy (*Primula malacoides*)
Snapdragon (*Antirrhinum*)
Spider plant (*Cleome spinosa*)
Stock (*Matthiola*)
Strawflower (*Helichrysum bracteatum*)
Sunrays (*Helipterum roseum*)

Sweet alyssum (*Lobularia maritima*)
Sweet pea (*Lathyrus odoratus*)
Sweet william (*Dianthus barbatus*)
Vervain (*Verbena*)
Vinca, or periwinkle (*Vinca rosea*)
Zinnia (*Zinnia elegans*)

Purple, Lavender, Lilac

Baby snapdragon (*Linaria faucicola*)
Bachelor's button, or cornflower (*Centaurea cyanus*)
Browallia
Butterfly flower (*Schizanthus*)
Candytuft, common (*Iberis umbellata*)
Candytuft, rocket (*Iberis amara*)
Canterbury bells (*Campanula medium*)
China aster (*Callistephus chinensis*)
Chrysanthemum
Clarkia
Dahlia
English daisy (*Bellis perennis*)
Farewell-to-spring, or godetia (*Godetia amoena*)
Four o'clock (*Mirabilis jalapa*)
Foxglove (*Digitalis purpurea*)
Heliotrope (*Heliotropium*)
Hollyhock (*Althaea rosea*)
Impatiens, or balsam (*Impatiens balsamina*)
Lantana
Larkspur (*Consolida ambigua*)

Love-in-a-mist, or nigella (*Nigella damascena*)
Lupine (*Lupinus hartwegii*)
Morning glory (*Ipomoea purpurea*)
Nemesia
Nicotiana
Painted tongue (*Salpiglossis sinuata*)
Pansy (*Viola wittrockiana*)
Petunia
Phlox (*Phlox drummondii*)
Pincushion flower (*Scabiosa atropurpurea*)
Pink (*Dianthus*)
Portulaca, or rose moss, or sun moss (*Portulaca grandiflora*)
Ragwort, purple (*Senecio elegans*)
Sea lavender, or statice (*Limonium*)
Snapdragon (*Antirrhinum*)
Stock (*Matthiola*)
Sweet alyssum (*Lobularia maritima*)
Sweet pea (*Lathyrus odoratus*)
Vervain (*Verbena*)
Viper's bugloss (*Echium*)
Wishbone flower (*Torenia*)
Zinnia (*Zinnia elegans*)

Red

Baby snapdragon (*Linaria faucicola*)
Begonia, wax (*Begonia semperflorens cultorum*)
Blanket flower, or gaillardia (*Gaillardia pulchella*)
Butterfly flower (*Schizanthus*)

California poppy (*Eschscholzia californica*)
Candytuft, common (*Iberis umbellata*)
Candytuft, rocket (*Iberis amara*)
Carnation (*Dianthus caryophyllus*)
China aster (*Callistephus chinensis*)
Chrysanthemum
Clarkia
Cockscomb (*Celosia argentea*)
Cosmos
Dahlia
English daisy (*Bellis perennis*)
Farewell-to-spring, or godetia (*Godetia amoena*)
Four o'clock (*Mirabilis jalapa*)
Foxglove (*Digitalis purpurea*)
Geranium, or pelargonium (*Pelargonium*)
Globe amaranth (*Gomphrena globosa*)
Hollyhock (*Althaea rosea*)
Impatiens, or balsam (*Impatiens balsamina*)
Lantana
Mignonette (*Reseda odorata*)
Nasturtium (*Tropaeolum*)
Nemesia
Nicotiana
Painted tongue (*Salpiglossis sinuata*)
Pansy (*Viola wittrockiana*)
Petunia
Phlox (*Phlox drummondii*)
Pink (*Dianthus*)
Poppy, Shirley (*Papaver rhoeas*)
Portulaca, or rose moss, or sun moss (*Portulaca grandiflora*)
Salvia, or scarlet sage (*Salvia splendens*)
Snapdragon (*Antirrhinum*)
Strawflower (*Helichrysum bracteatum*)
Sunrays (*Helipterum roseum*)
Sweet william (*Dianthus barbatus*)
Tickseed, or calliopsis (*Coreopsis*)
Vervain (*Verbena*)
Zinnia (*Zinnia elegans*)

White

Acroclinium (*Helipterum manglesii*)
African daisy (*Arctotis*)
Baby's breath (*Gypsophila elegans*)
Baby snapdragon (*Linaria faucicola*)
Bachelor's button, or cornflower (*Centaurea cyanus*)
Begonia, wax (*Begonia semperflorens cultorum*)
Browallia
Butterfly flower (*Schizanthus*)
Candytuft, common (*Iberis umbellata*)
Candytuft, rocket (*Iberis amara*)
Canterbury bells (*Campanula medium*)
Cape marigold (*Dimorphotheca pluvialis*)
Carnation (*Dianthus caryophyllus*)
China aster (*Callistephus chinensis*)
Chrysanthemum
Clarkia
Cosmos

Dahlia
Dwarf morning glory, or convolvulus (*Convolvulus tricolor*)
English daisy (*Bellis perennis*)
Evening primrose (*Oenothera biennis*)
Farewell-to-spring, or godetia (*Godetia amoena*)
Flossflower, or ageratum (*Ageratum houstonianum*)
Forget-me-not (*Myosotis sylvatica*)
Four o'clock (*Mirabilis jalapa*)
Foxglove (*Digitalis purpurea*)
Geranium, or pelargonium (*Pelargonium*)
Globe amaranth (*Gomphrena globosa*)
Hollyhock (*Althaea rosea*)
Impatiens, or balsam (*Impatiens balsamina*)
Lantana
Larkspur (*Consolida ambigua*)
Lobelia, edging (*Lobelia erinus*)
Love-in-a-mist, or nigella (*Nigella damascena*)
Lupine (*Lupinus hartwegii*)
Mignonette (*Reseda odorata*)
Morning glory (*Ipomoea purpurea*)
Nemesia
Nicotiana
Pansy (*Viola wittrockiana*)
Petunia
Phlox (*Phlox drummondii*)
Pincushion flower (*Scabiosa atropurpurea*)
Pink (*Dianthus*)
Poppy, Shirley (*Papaver rhoeas*)
Portulaca, or rose moss, or sun moss (*Portulaca

grandiflora*)
Primrose, fairy (*Primula malacoides*)
Sea lavender, or statice (*Limonium*)
Snapdragon (*Antirrhinum*)
Spider plant (*Cleome spinosa*)
Stock (*Matthiola*)
Strawflower (*Helichrysum bracteatum*)
Sunrays (*Helipterum roseum*)
Sweet alyssum (*Lobularia maritima*)
Sweet pea (*Lathyrus odoratus*)
Sweet william (*Dianthus barbatus*)
Vervain (*Verbena*)
Vinca, or periwinkle (*Vinca rosea*)
Zinnia (*Zinnia elegans*)

Yellow

African daisy (*Arctotis*)
Baby snapdragon (*Linaria faucicola*)
Blanket flower, or gaillardia (*Gaillardia pulchella*)
California poppy (*Eschscholzia californica*)
Cape marigold (*Dimorphotheca pluvialis*)
Carnation (*Dianthus caryophyllus*)
China aster (*Callistephus chinensis*)
Chrysanthemum
Cockscomb (*Celosia argentea*)
Cosmos
Dahlia
Four o'clock (*Mirabilis jalapa*)
Hollyhock (*Althaea rosea*)

Lantana
Marigold (*Tagetes*)
Mignonette (*Reseda odorata*)
Nasturtium (*Tropaeolum*)
Nemesia
Painted tongue (*Salpiglossis sinuata*)
Pansy (*Viola wittrockiana*)
Poppy, Shirley (*Papaver rhoeas*)
Portulaca, or rose moss, or sun moss (*Portulaca grandiflora*)
Pot marigold (*Calendula officinalis*)

Sea lavender, or statice (*Limonium*)
Snapdragon (*Antirrhinum*)
Stock (*Matthiola*)
Strawflower (*Helichrysum bracteatum*)
Sunflower (*Helianthus*)
Sunrays (*Helipterum roseum*)
Tickseed, or calliopsis (*Coreopsis*)
Transvaal daisy (*Gerbera jamesonii*)
Wishbone flower (*Torenia*)
Zinnia (*Zinnia elegans*)

PERENNIALS

Blue

Anemone, Japanese (*Anemone japonica*)
Aster, hardy; or Michaelmas daisy (*Aster novi-belgii*)
Balloon flower (*Platycodon grandiflorus*)
Bellflower, or campanula (*Campanula*)
Bluebells, Virginia (*Mertensia virginica*)
Blue marguerite (*Felicia amelloides*)
Bugloss, or anchusa (*Anchusa azurea*)
Columbine (*Aquilegia*)
Delphinium
Flax (*Linum perenne*)
Forget-me-not (*Myosotis scorpioides*)

Geranium, or storksbill geranium (*Geranium*)
Globe thistle (*Echinops exaltatus*)
Iris
Lupine (*Lupinus*)
Moss pink (*Phlox subulata*)
Phlox, garden (*Phlox paniculata*)
Plantain lily (*Hosta*)
Primrose (*Primula*)
Salvia, or sage (*Salvia*)
Speedwell, or veronica (*Veronica*)
Stokes' aster, or stokesia (*Stokesia laevis*)
Viola

Bronze

Blanket flower, or gaillardia (*Gaillardia aristata*)

Chrysanthemum
Gloriosa daisy (*Rudbeckia*)
Sneezeweed (*Helenium autumnale*)
Viola

Orange

Aster, hardy; or Michaelmas daisy (*Aster novi-belgii*)
Blanket flower, or gaillardia (*Gaillardia aristata*)
Butterflyweed (*Asclepias tuberosa*)
Chrysanthemum
Coneflower, or rudbeckia (*Rudbeckia*)
Daylily (*Hemerocallis*)
Lupine (*Lupinus*)
Phlox, garden (*Phlox paniculata*)
Pink (*Dianthus*)
Poppy, Iceland (*Papaver nudicaule*)
Poppy, oriental (*Papaver orientale*)
Red-hot poker, or kniphofia, or tritoma (*Kniphofia*)
Sedum, or stonecrop (*Sedum*)
Sunflower (*Helianthus*)
Viola

Pink, Rose

Anemone (*Anemone japonica*)
Aster, hardy; or Michaelmas daisy (*Aster novi-belgii*)

Astilbe, or spiraea (*Astilbe arendsii*)
Baby's breath (*Gypsophila paniculata*)
Balloon flower (*Platycodon grandiflorus*)
Beardtongue (*Penstemon*)
Bee balm, or bergamot (*Monarda didyma*)
Bellflower (*Campanula*)
Bleeding heart (*Dicentra spectabilis*)
Candytuft, edging (*Iberis sempervirens*)
Chrysanthemum
Columbine (*Aquilegia*)
Coralbells, or alumroot (*Heuchera sanguinea*)
Delphinium
Gas plant (*Dictamnus albus*)
Gayfeather (*Liatris*)
Geranium, or storksbill geranium (*Geranium*)
Hibiscus, or rose mallow (*Hibiscus moscheutos*)
Lenten rose, or helleborus (*Helleborus orientalis*)
Loosestrife (*Lythrum*)
Lupine (*Lupinus*)
Moss pink (*Phlox subulata*)
Painted daisy (*Chrysanthemum coccineum*)
Peony (*Paeonia*)
Phlox, garden (*Phlox paniculata*)
Pink (*Dianthus*)
Poppy, Iceland (*Papaver nudicaule*)
Poppy, oriental (*Papaver orientale*)
Primrose (*Primula*)
Sedum, or stonecrop (*Sedum*)
Speedwell, or veronica (*Veronica*)
Thrift (*Armeria*)

Tickseed (*Coreopsis*)
Viola

Thrift (*Armeria*)
Viola

Purple, Lavender, Lilac

Anemone, japanese (*Anemone japonica*)
Aster, hardy; or Michaelmas daisy (*Aster novi-belgii*)
Balloon flower (*Platycodon grandiflorus*)
Bee balm, or bergamot (*Monarda didyma*)
Catmint (*Nepeta mussinii*)
Christmas rose, or helleborus (*Helleborus niger*)
Chrysanthemum
Columbine (*Aquilegia*)
Delphinium
Gayfeather (*Liatris*)
Geranium, or storksbill geranium (*Geranium*)
Iris
Lenten rose, or helleborus (*Helleborus orientalis*)
Loosestrife (*Lythrum*)
Lupine (*Lupinus*)
Moss pink (*Phlox subulata*)
Peony (*Paeonia*)
Phlox, garden (*Phlox paniculata*)
Pink (*Dianthus*)
Plantain lily (*Hosta*)
Primrose (*Primula*)
Salvia, or sage (*Salvia*)
Sedum, or stonecrop (*Sedum*)
Stokes' aster, or stokesia (*Stokesia laevis*)

Red

Anemone, Japanese (*Anemone japonica*)
Aster, hardy; or Michaelmas daisy (*Aster novi-belgii*)
Astilbe, or spiraea (*Astilbe arendsii*)
Beardtongue (*Penstemon*)
Bee balm, or bergamot (*Monarda didyma*)
Blanket flower, or gaillardia (*Gaillardia aristata*)
Bleeding heart (*Dicentra spectabilis*)
Chrysanthemum
Columbine (*Aquilegia*)
Coralbells, or alumroot (*Heuchera sanguinea*)
Daylily (*Hemerocallis*)
Geranium, or storksbill geranium (*Geranium*)
Hibiscus, or rose mallow (*Hibiscus moscheutos*)
Iris, Japanese (*Iris kaempferi*)
Lenten rose, or helleborus (*Helleborus orientalis*)
Lobelia, or cardinal flower (*Lobelia cardinalis*)
Loosestrife (*Lythrum*)
Lupine (*Lupinus*)
Moss pink (*Phlox subulata*)
Painted daisy (*Chrysanthemum coccineum*)
Peony (*Paeonia*)
Phlox, garden (*Phlox paniculata*)
Pink (*Dianthus*)
Poppy, oriental (*Papaver orientale*)

Red-hot poker, or kniphofia, or tritoma (*Kniphofia*)
Sedum, or stonecrop (*Sedum*)
Sneezeweed (*Helenium autumnale*)
Viola
Yarrow (*Achillea*)

White

Anemone, Japanese (*Anemone japonica*)
Aster, hardy; or Michaelmas daisy (*Aster novibelgii*)
Astilbe, or spiraea (*Astilbe arendsii*)
Baby's breath (*Gypsophila paniculata*)
Balloon flower (*Platycodon grandiflorus*)
Bee balm, or bergamot (*Monarda didyma*)
Bellflower, or campanula (*Campanula*)
Bleeding heart (*Dicentra spectabilis*)
Candytuft, edging (*Iberis sempervirens*)
Christmas rose, or helleborus (*Helleborus niger*)
Chrysanthemum
Columbine (*Aquilegia*)
Coralbells, or alumroot (*Heuchera sanguinea*)
Daylily (*Hemerocallis*)
Delphinium
Gas plant (*Dictamnus albus*)
Gayfeather (*Liatris*)
Geranium, or storksbill geranium (*Geranium*)
Hibiscus, or rose mallow (*Hibiscus moscheutos*)
Iris

Lenten rose, or helleborus (*Helleborus orientalis*)
Lily-of-the-valley (*Convallaria majalis*)
Lupine (*Lupinus*)
Meadowsweet (*Filipendula vulgaris*)
Moss pink (*Phlox subulata*)
Painted daisy (*Chrysanthemum coccineum*)
Peony (*Paeonia*)
Phlox, garden (*Phlox paniculata*)
Pink (*Dianthus*)
Plantain lily (*Hosta*)
Poppy, Iceland (*Papaver nudicaule*)
Poppy, oriental (*Papaver orientale*)
Primrose (*Primula*)
Shasta daisy (*Chrysanthemum maximum*)
Speedwell, or veronica (*Veronica*)
Stokes' aster, or stokesia (*Stokesia laevis*)
Thrift (*Armeria*)
Yarrow (*Achillea*)
Yucca

Yellow

Adonis (*Adonis vernalis*)
Aster, hardy; or Michaelmas daisy (*Aster novibelgii*)
Basket-of-gold, or alyssum (*Alyssum saxatile*)
Blanket flower, or gaillardia (*Gaillardia aristata*)
Chrysanthemum
Columbine (*Aquilegia*)
Coneflower, or rudbeckia (*Rudbeckia*)

Daylily (*Hemerocallis*)
Evening primrose (*Oenothera*)
Feverfew (*Chrysanthemum parthenium*)
Globeflower (*Trollius europaeus*)
Gloriosa daisy (*Rudbeckia*)
Golden marguerite, or anthemis (*Anthemis tinctoria*)
Leopard's bane (*Doronicum*)
Lupine (*Lupinus*)
Poppy, Iceland (*Papaver nudicaule*)
Primrose (*Primula*)

Red-hot poker, or kniphofia, or tritoma (*Kniphofia*)
Sedum, or stonecrop (*Sedum*)
Sneezeweed (*Helenium autumnale*)
Spurge (*Euphorbia*)
Sunflower (*Helianthus*)
Thermopsis, or Carolina lupine (*Thermopsis caroliniana*)
Tickseed (*Coreopsis*)
Viola
Yarrow (*Achillea*)

EXTENDING THE GARDEN CALENDAR: ORNAMENTAL FRUIT, COLORFUL FOLIAGE

FRUIT

Black

Barberry (*Berberis*, many species and hybrids)
Chokeberry, black (*Aronia melanocarpa*)
Cotoneaster, Peking (*Cotoneaster acutifolius*)
Elder, American (*Sambucus canadensis*)
Haw, black (*Viburnum prunifolium*)
Holly, Japanese (*Ilex crenata*)
Honeysuckle, Hall's Japanese (*Lonicera japonica halliana*)
Indian hawthorn (*Raphiolepsis indica*)
Mahonia, creeping (*Mahonia repens*)
Privet (*Ligustrum*, many species and hybrids)
Viburnum, siebold (*Viburnum sieboldii*)
Wayfaring tree (*Viburnum lantana*)

Blue, Purple

Arrowwood (*Viburnum dentatum*)
Blueberry, highbush (*Vaccinium corymbosum*)
Boston ivy, or Japanese creeper (*Parthenocissus tricuspidata*)
Callicarpa (*Callicarpa bodinieri*)
Chokeberry, purple (*Aronia prunifolia*)
Dogwood, blue (*Cornus alternifolia*)
Holly grape (*Mahonia aquifolium*)
Honeysuckle, box (*Lonicera nitida*)
Japanese aralia (*Fatsia japonica*)

Privet, border (*Ligustrum obtusifolium*)
Viburnum, david (*Viburnum davidii*)
Wintergreen, veitch (*Gaultheria veitchiana*)

Orange, Yellow

Bittersweet, oriental (*Celastrus orbiculatus*)
Chinaberry tree (*Melia azedarach*)
Daphne, rose (*Daphne cneorum*)
Euonymus, Japanese (*Euonymus japonica*)
Fire thorn (*Pyracantha*, many species and hybrids)
Honeysuckle, tatarian (*Lonicera tatarica*)
Sea buckthorn (*Hippophae rhamnoides*)
Winter creeper, or evergreen bittersweet (*Euonymus fortunei*)

Red

Ardisia (*Ardisia crispa*)
Barberry, common (*Berberis vulgaris*)
Barberry, Japanese (*Berberis thunbergii*)
Barberry, Korean (*Berberis koreana*)
Barberry, mentor (*Berberis mentorensis*)
Bearberry (*Arctostaphylos uva-ursi*)
Bittersweet, American (*Celastrus scandens*)
Ceanothus, inland (*Ceanothus ovatus*)
Chokeberry, red (*Aronia arbutifolia*)
Coralberry, chenault (*Symphoricarpos chenaultii*)
Cornelian, cherry (*Cornus mas*)
Cotoneaster (many species and hybrids)
Crab apple, sargent (*Malus sargentii*)

Daphne, february (*Daphne mezereum*)
Dogwood (*Cornus*, many species and hybrids)
Elaeagnus, cherry (*Elaeagnus multiflora*)
Euonymus (many species and hybrids)
Fire thorn (*Pyracantha*, many species and hybrids)
Hawthorn (*Crataegus*, many species and hybrids)
Heavenly, or sacred, bamboo (*Nandina domestica*)
Holly (*Ilex*, many species and hybrids)
Honeysuckle, Amur (*Lonicera maackii*)
Honeysuckle, tatarian (*Lonicera tatarica*)
Honeysuckle, trumpet (*Lonicera sempervirens*)
Honeysuckle, winter (*Lonicera fragrantissima*)
Japanese laurel (*Aucuba japonica*)
Kadsura, scarlet (*Kadsura japonica*)
Magnolia, star (*Magnolia stellata*)
Mountain ash, European (*Sorbus aucuparia*)
Photinia, Chinese (*Photinia serrulata*)
Rose (*Rosa*, many species and hybrids)
Sarcococca, fragrant (*Sarcococca ruscifolia*)
Skimmia, Japanese (*Skimmia japonica*)
Skimmia, reeves (*Skimmia reevesiana*)
Sumac (*Rhus*, many species and hybrids)
Viburnum (many species and hybrids)
Yew, Japanese (*Taxus cuspidata*)

AUTUMN FOLIAGE

Bronze

Bearberry (*Arctostaphylos uva-ursi*)

Fetterbush (*Leucothoë catesbaei*)
Holly grape (*Mahonia aquifolium*)

Orange, Yellow

Arrowwood (*Viburnum dentatum*)
Bellflower, or enkianthus (*Enkianthus campanulatus*)
Five-leaved aralia (*Acanthopanax sieboldianus*)
Fothergilla
Fringe tree (*Chionanthus virginicus*)
Ginkgo, or maidenhair tree (*Ginkgo biloba*)
Katsura tree (*Cercidiphyllum japonicum*)
Larch, European (*Larix decidua*)
Maple, Norway (*Acer platanoides*)
Maple, red (*Acer rubrum*)
Maple, sugar (*Acer saccharum*)
Pignut (*Carya glabra*)
Spiraea, bridal-wreath (*Spiraea prunifolia*)
Spiraea, thunberg (*Spiraea thunbergii*)
Tulip tree (*Liriodendron tulipifera*)
Witch hazel (*Hamamelis*)
Yellowwood (*Cladrastis lutea*)

Purple

Ash, white (*Fraxinus americana*)
Dogwood, gray (*Cornus racemosa*)
Sweet gum (*Liquidambar styraciflua*)
Viburnum (several species and hybrids)

Red

Azalea, Kaempfer (*Rhododendron obtusum kaempferi*)
Azalea, Korean (*Rhododendron mucronulatum*)
Barberry (*Berberis*, many species and hybrids)
Blueberry, highbush (*Vaccinium corymbosum*)
Chokeberry, red (*Aronia arbutifolia*)
Currant, alpine (*Ribes alpinum*)
Dogwood, flowering (*Cornus florida*)
Bellflower, or enkianthus (*Enkianthus campanulatus*)
Euonymus, winged; or winged spindle tree (*Euonymus alata*)
Heavenly, or sacred, bamboo (*Nandina domestica*)
Hydrangea, oak-leaved (*Hydrangea quercifolia*)
Maple, Amur (*Acer ginnala*)

Maple, Japanese (*Acer palmatum*)
Maple, red (*Acer rubrum*)
Maple, sugar (*Acer saccharum*)
Maple, vine (*Acer circinatum*)
Photinia, Chinese (*Photinia serrulata*)
Oak, pin (*Quercus palustris*)
Oak, scarlet (*Quercus coccinea*)
Rock spray (*Cotoneaster horizontalis*)
Serviceberry, shadblow (*Amelanchier canadensis*)
Sourwood, or sorrel tree (*Oxydendrum arboreum*)
Sumac (*Rhus*, several species and hybrids)
Sweet gum (*Liquidambar styraciflua*)
Tupelo, or pepperidge, or sour gum (*Nyssa sylvatica*)
Washington thorn (*Crataegus phaenopyrum*)
Viburnum (several species and hybrids)

PESTS AND DISEASES OF
FLOWERING PLANTS

INSECTS OR DISEASE	DESCRIPTION	CONTROLS
Aphids	These small, ovoid insects feed on foliage and stems, weakening plants, causing leaves to curl.	Hose off or spray plants with malathion.
Aster wilts	Streaks appear on stems, and plants droop, wither, and die. Insect damage or bacteria, viruses, or fungi may be the cause.	Use resistant varieties. Destroy infected plants. Practice plant rotation. If you suspect a fungus, apply a fungicide.
Aster yellows	This disease, resulting in stunted growth, is caused by virus carried by leafhoppers and aphids.	Destroy infected plants. Ladybugs will attack the carriers.
Bacterial wilts	Plants suddenly wilt and die.	Bacteria that cause disease persist in soil, so remove all parts of infected plants and practice plant rotation.
Basal rot	After a fungus attacks bulb through roots, plant becomes stunted and stems wilt and die.	Disease exists in soil, so plant resistant varieties, rotate plantings, destroy infected plants. Apply a fungicide.
Blister beetles	These long-legged, black-to-grey, inch-long insects with yellow stripes eat foliage and flowers.	Pick bugs off by hand (wear gloves), dust plants with lime and flour, or spray with malathion or pyrethrum.

INSECTS OR DISEASE	DESCRIPTION	CONTROLS
Borers	These pests tunnel through stems and branches, causing them to wilt and topple.	Use light traps to collect borer moths.
Botrytis leaf blight	Small, round, orange-red spots appear on leaves; foliage dies.	A fungus is the cause, so select growing sites with good air circulation and good drainage. Apply a fungicide.
Botrytis petal blight	A fungus deforms flowers.	Provide adequate ventilation. Apply a fungicide. Keep growing area moderately dry.
Botrytis rhizome rot	Soft, foul-smelling rot in rhizomes is caused by fungi.	Plant only healthy rhizomes. Apply a fungicide. Destroy infected plants.
Caterpillars	These insects chew foliage.	Stinkbugs eat caterpillar beetles in immature stage. Apply potion of ground pepper and boiling water to soil, pick off bugs by hand, or spray with malathion.
Chrysanthemum stunt	Flowers are small, leaves pale green or reddish.	This viral disease is carried in planting stock; buy only from reputable dealers.

INSECTS OR DISEASE	DESCRIPTION	CONTROLS
Color breakdown	Streaks or blotches mar flower color (especially common in tulips and gladiolus).	Destroy diseased plants to eliminate aphids, which spread the virus.
Crown and root rot	Plants weaken, discolor, wilt, frequently die.	A fungus is the cause, so be sure soil is well drained. Sterilize soil before planting. Apply a fungicide. Destroy infected plants. Rotate plantings.
Cucumber beetles	These spotted or striped insects destroy foliage.	Apply potion of ground pepper and boiling water to soil.
Cyclamen mites	These white, microscopic insects cause distorted leaves, blackened buds.	Mites travel fast, so keep plants well spaced to avoid infestation. Apply rotenone, if necessary.
Damping off	Attacked by fungus, stems of seedlings collapse and rot off at soil surface.	Avoid excessive moisture and crowding. Water sparingly.
Flea beetles	These black insects chew holes in foliage.	Destroy debris in and around area so pests cannot overwinter.

INSECTS OR DISEASE	DESCRIPTION	CONTROLS
Gall midges	Larvae of tiny gnats form cone-shaped galls in chrysanthemums, their only host, causing twisted stems and distorted buds.	Burn infected plants.
Gladiolus thrips	These minute insects distort flower buds and cause streaks in foliage.	Plant bulbs in early fall, if that is possible in your area. Remove infested buds and blossoms. Rotate plantings.
Gray mold	Oval or circular spots, caused by fungus, appear on leaves.	Thin out plants. Destroy affected parts. Provide good air circulation. Apply a fungicide.
Ground mealybugs	Smaller than mealybugs, these insects live off roots in soil.	Use healthy cuttings and rotate plantings. Move plants and dry out soil bed for a month after an attack.
Japanese beetles	These iridescent insects with metallic green, copper, and brown wings feed on foliage and flowers.	Apply Doom (trade name), which infects insects with milky spore disease.
Leaf and bud nematodes	These tiny wormlike pests attack many plants, including chrysanthemums and lilies. Yellow wedge-shaped spots appear; leaves dry up and fall.	Remove and burn infected plants. Maintain high-humus soil. Rotate plantings.

INSECTS OR DISEASE	DESCRIPTION	CONTROLS
Leafhoppers	These small, greenish yellow, wedge-shaped insects eat foliage.	Apply pyrethrum or quassia. Ladybugs will eat the pests.
Leaf spots	Black spots appear on leaves, stems, and buds.	Bacteria overwinter on dead leaves and crowns of infected plants, so keep area scrupulously clean.
Nematodes	These worms attack roots, producing knots or swellings; plants wilt, become stunted.	Maintain high-humus soil.
Powdery mildews	White powdery spots, caused by fungi, appear on foliage.	Dry out soil somewhat. Apply a fungicide. Keep growing area clear of weeds.
Rusts	Brown pustules, caused by fungi, appear on leaves and stems. Leaves dry up and fall.	Plant resistant varieties. Maintain good humus content in soil. Apply a fungicide.
Slugs, snails	These pests eat holes in leaves at night.	Use Snarol (trade name) without metaldehyde. Set out shallow containers of beer to trap them.

BIBLIOGRAPHY

Bush-Brown, James and Louise. *America's Garden Book*. Rev. ed. New York: Charles Scribner's Sons, 1979.

Royal Horticultural Society. *Dictionary of Gardening: A Practical and Scientific Encyclopedia of Horticulture*. Ed. Fred J. Chittenden. 4 vols. London and New York: Oxford University Press, 1965.

Wilson, Helen Van Pelt. *Helen Van Pelt Wilson's Own Garden and Landscape Book*. New York: Doubleday, 1973.

Wright, Walter P., ed. *A History of Garden Art*. Trans. Mrs. Archer-Hind. 2 vols. New York: Hacker Art Books, 1966.

INDEX